The Miracle of the Seventh-day Ox

Bradley Booth

REVIEW AND HERALD® PUBLISHING ASSOCIATION
Since 1861 | www.reviewandherald.com

Other books by Bradley Booth:
Dare to Stand Alone
Plagues in the Palace
Prince of Dreams
The Prodigal
Seventh-day Ox and Other Stories
Shepherd Warrior
They Call Him the Miracle Man
Time Warp

To order, call 1-800-765-6955. Visit us at www.reviewandherald.com for information on other Review and Herald® products.

Copyright © 2012 by Review and Herald® Publishing Association

Published by Review and Herald® Publishing Association

The Review and Herald® Publishing Association publishes biblically based materials for spiritual, physical, and mental growth and Christian discipleship.

The author assumes full responsibility for the accuracy of all facts and quotations as cited in this book.

Texts credited to NKJV are from the New King James Version. Copyright © 1979, 1980, 1982 by Thomas Nelson, Inc. Used by permission. All rights reserved.

This book was
Edited by Kalie Kelch
Copyedited by Judy Blodgett
Designed by Emily Ford
Cover art by © Thinkstock.com
Typeset: Minion Pro 10/12

Printed by Pacific Press® Publishing Association
PRINTED IN CHINA

Library of Congress Cataloging-in-Publication Data
Booth, Bradley, 1957- .
  [Excerpted from] The seventh-day ox, and other miracle stories from Russia / Bradley Booth.
    p. cm.
1. Seventh-Day Adventists—Soviet Union. 2. Animals—Religious aspects—Seventh-Day Adventists. 3. Miracles—Soviet Union. I. Title.
  BX6153.4.S65B66 2011
  286.7'47--dc22

                    2010011258

ISBN 978-0-8280-2640-6

February 2022

Chapter 1

Nickolai Panchuk stared at the four walls of the jail cell around him. The cold gray concrete made him feel as if he were in a tomb—cold and frightened and alone.

What would become of him? What was to be his fate? He had refused to cooperate with the KGB[1] thus far—refused to betray the whereabouts of yet another fledgling church he had helped organize only a month ago. It wasn't a large church—just a company of believers in the city of Kiev, the capital of the Ukraine—but Nickolai had refused to turn over a list of the members to the KGB.

And who could blame him? The gospel message was spreading so fast that every few months Nickolai was forming yet another company of believers. At present he was shepherd and pastor of 11 such congregations.

Groups typically met to worship in houses and cellars and barns, but 15 or 20 members seemed to be the magic number before the group was considered too large. The places they met were just too small to hold more than that number. And everyone loved the close-knit family feeling they experienced from being part of a company of Seventh-day Adventist Christians.

Nickolai leaned back against the cold wall of the prison cell and closed his eyes. The peace that came from worshipping with like believers was more than enough pay for the pain and hardship he had faced during the past few months. It wasn't easy, but he was getting used to it. Five times now the KGB had cornered him to find out information about the Seventh-day Adventist Church members who were meeting in scattered companies in the towns and small villages of the area. Twice they had come to his house, and three times they had used a public confrontation to humiliate him and try to make him talk.

The KGB needed that crucial list of church members. Without it everything was a hit-and-miss operation for them—like sifting for needles in the chaff of a haystack.

Fortunately for Nickolai, the KGB in the area where he lived were decent enough to leave his family out of it. Other pastors in Russia had not been so lucky. Nickolai had heard terrible stories of what the KGB sometimes did to get pastors to talk.

But Nickolai always remained steadfast and determined in his promise to leave everything in God's hands. His faith was strong. He would not betray the church members and their trust no matter what the cost to himself or his family.

But this time the interrogation process was different— it was obvious the KGB had something else in mind for Nickolai. When he had first arrived at the KGB headquarters, they had sat him in a chair and kept him awake for more than two days. They had used the proverbial bright lights in his eyes, shouting tactics, and even threats of where they might send him to help straighten him out.

But all to no avail. Nickolai had remained undaunted and unmovable. Their tactics did not intimidate him. Unfortunately, the KGB were more than persistent. They were determined! What was to come next was anybody's guess, though Nickolai felt it didn't take a rocket scientist to figure it out.

He was considered an enemy of the state. Christians were high on the list of rebels who needed to be reformed and retooled for society. If they could be punished enough, maybe they would finally see the light. Those were the words from the top on down, but Nickolai guessed that few in the upper ranks of the military ever bothered themselves about what actually happened to pastors such as Nickolai. As long as the KGB methods produced results, they cared little about the details.

Nickolai wondered what time it was. He had no watch, and the scant meals they brought him were the only indications that time was passing, though he was sure he had been in his cell for several days now. For Nickolai, time seemed to stand still.

Suddenly Nickolai heard footsteps coming down the long concrete corridor. The footsteps slowed and then stopped in front of his cell, and he could hear a hand fumbling with a key in the door. "On your feet!" a voice barked.

Nickolai scrambled to his feet in time to see a big burly figure fill the doorway. A lone 40-watt bulb burning in the corridor cast eerie shadows past the hulking frame. Nickolai assumed that the man was one of the guards who had been bringing him his meals since he had arrived.

"The boss wants to see you!"

Nickolai waited for the guard to give him specific orders, but the big man simply pulled him into the corridor and pushed him in the direction he wanted him to go.

They went up a flight of concrete stairs, and then down another hallway until they came to a big room with a large desk in it and two straight-backed chairs. Other than that, the only thing in the room was another lightbulb burning feebly high overhead.

Behind the desk sat an intimidating officer in a gray-green uniform—a manila folder lay open on the desk in front of him. He never bothered to raise his eyes when Nickolai walked in, but continued staring at the contents of the folder over horn-rimmed reading glasses. A shot glass and bottle of vodka sat on the desk beside him, and a long cigarette dangled from his clean-shaven mouth.

Nickolai remained standing, not daring to sit down in the second chair. Whatever was coming next would no doubt be better received standing up.

"Preacher man!" The officer threw out the expression he had been using on Nickolai for the past several days. "Have you given my proposition some more thought?" The

5

officer still did not look Nickolai in the eye, and Nickolai was grateful for it. Eye contact was a code of intimidation with the KGB. If a prisoner should respond to such a gesture with eye contact of his own, it was understood that the victim was ready to finally come to some kind of agreement.

And for Nickolai that was impossible. He knew he could never bring himself to agree to the KGB's terms that he reveal the list of the church members in his district! Never! Never in a thousand years!

But the officer was waiting, and Nickolai knew there was nothing for him to do except tell the "boss" exactly what he had told him before. His mind was made up—there would be no compromise, no "deal." For Nickolai there was no other choice, and he knew the officer would soon grow impatient because of it.

"I'm sorry, sir, but I can't comply. My God and my conscience won't allow it."

The officer pushed Nickolai's folder away and folded his arms across his chest. Nickolai kept his eyes fixed on the wall behind the officer's head, but he could tell that the man was staring at him over the tops of his glasses, and it made him nervous.

---

[1] The KGB (КГБ) was the commonly used acronym for the Russian Комитет государственной безопасности (Komitet gosudarstvennoy bezopasnosti, or Committee for State Security). It was the national security agency of the Soviet Union from 1954 until 1991, and was the premier internal security, intelligence, and secret police organization during that time.

[2] The state security agency of the republic of Belarus currently uses the Russian name KGB. While most of the KGB archives remain classified, two online documentary sources are available.

Chapter 2

I s that all you have to say for yourself?" the KGB officer growled. Nickolai hesitated for only a moment. "Sir! That is my final decision."

The officer shook his head. "You're serious, aren't you?" He took the cigarette from his mouth and tapped a long string of ashes onto the floor.

"I am, sir."

"You are a stubborn man." The officer shook his head again and sighed in frustration. "We've used all the usual methods and forms of diplomacy we know." He put the cigarette back into his mouth and took another long drag from it. "I wish you were on our side, preacher man. It would make my job so much easier."

Preacher man. Nickolai dared to smile at the nickname the officer had given him. And *diplomacy?* Their process of interrogation was anything but diplomatic. Victims of the KGB had choices, all right, but they were very one-sided. Either allow yourself to be persuaded and comply, or else pay the piper.

The officer finished his cigarette and poured a shot glass of vodka. Surprisingly he extended the glass in Nickolai's direction, but Nickolai declined with a simple "Thank you, sir, but I don't drink."

The officer grunted and set the glass down roughly, spilling half of the vodka on the file folder in front of him. His mood quickly turned from warm to sour.

"Well, I can see that I'm getting nowhere fast, preacher man. I've got more important things to do than waste my time here with you!" he raised his voice. "I might as well be talking to the wall for all the good this conversation is doing!

"We've kept you awake, hammering at you incessantly, but you won't break! We've offered you bribes and positions in our organization! We've even been willing to concede some of the restrictions we've put on you during past encounters, but you always give us the same answer! It's obvious you're going to be of no help here!"

The officer raised a hand to shake his finger at Nickolai. "I'm tired of this nonsense! We were hoping to talk to you and make some sense out of this whole situation, but I can see that you are more stubborn than ever."

He pulled a handkerchief from his uniform pocket and sopped up the spilled vodka before closing the manila folder. "Your case is out of my hands. My superiors expect results, and if I can't get them, then there's going to be a price to pay."

His voice grew calm again. "I like you, Nickolai, but if we can't come to an agreement, there is nothing I can do to save you." It was the first time he had used Nickolai's name since Nickolai had first come to the prison five days before.

"I've been instructed to inform you that you are being sentenced to labor in a prison camp in Siberia. Unless you are ready to answer our questions, there is nothing more I can do."

To Nickolai's surprise, the officer stood to his feet and extended his hand. "Good luck, preacher man. May your God be with you." He gestured toward the door, nodded to the guard, and then sat down again to finish his paperwork.

As Nickolai turned to go, he thought he saw a look of pity in the KGB officer's eyes, but he knew he must be mistaken. KGB officers were known for their hard hearts and their unflinching determination to get information out of their victims.

Nickolai was led back to his cell. As the door clanged shut behind him, he took stock of his situation. Things were not looking good. There was no doubt that he had made the right decision, but at what cost? He had no idea how long he would be sentenced to the frigid wastelands of Siberia. Years? Decades? Until he died?

He cringed as he thought of the dreaded sentence so frightening to any prisoner's ears—banishment to the Siberian frontier. Summer temperatures in Siberia could be cool and damp, with swarms of black flies and huge, bloodthirsty mosquitoes everywhere. And with no towns or settlements in that vast wasteland, he had heard that escape was impossible. There was little chance of survival should a prisoner even attempt to make an escape.

But it was the winters in Siberia that were the most fearsome for a prisoner. Temperatures sometimes dropped to 50 degrees below zero, and with the biting wind that chased its way across the northland, living conditions were unthinkable.

Nickolai shivered in his cell just thinking about the prospects of such a future. There was still time for him to rethink the whole thing, time to change his mind and escape the fate he had been handed.

But of course Nickolai knew that he would never do that. He could not. It was against everything he had ever believed in and stood for all his life. Allegiance to the Higher Power in his life was the most important thing now. The Russian KGB could take away his pulpit. They could take away his freedom and even his health, but they would never take away his choice to serve God and be true to Him.

And now at the recommendation of the secret police, the Communist government was going to exile him to an outpost prison in Siberia. It was a heavy price to pay, but Nickolai had no doubt in his mind that God was going to be with him.

He would not give up his resolve to guard his church members' names. He would continue to speak for God no matter where he lived. He would witness for God no matter what it cost him.

And who knew? Maybe the Holy Spirit would use him to do even greater things for God than he was already doing. Time would tell.

Chapter 3

Nickolai awoke with a start as he felt the engineer apply the air brakes to the line of train cars. The sun was not yet up, but streaks of magenta were creasing the horizon as Nickolai stared sleepily out the train car windows. Just a few hours before, the gentle swaying of the train had lulled him into a fitful sleep. Handcuffed to the seat, he had found it difficult to stretch out in a comfortable position.

He sat up stiffly and noticed that most of the other passengers were still sleeping. Some were stretched out on upper bunks, some across the lower seats as he was, while still others were sprawled in the aisles on the floor.

The previous afternoon two army soldiers had boarded the train with Nickolai and two other prisoners and set out for the city of Omsk. They knew little as to the details of their journey, except that they would eventually end up at a Siberian prison camp.

Nickolai tried to remain positive in spite of his uncomfortable surroundings, which included being handcuffed at all times, except for when he needed to use the bathroom (and even then, a guard stood outside the door). It wasn't much, but Nickolai was grateful for the small bag of bread and can of water the prisoners received each day. The rations were meager, but as the train chugged eastward along the tracks, Nickolai's mind kept returning to a familiar verse in Scripture: "Even your bread and water shall be sure." The words to the text comforted him when he thought about the literal fulfillment of that promise.

The trip was tedious, but Nickolai knew that even on

this train he should be ready to speak for God and witness for his faith. Somewhere during that first morning on the train Nickolai struck up a conversation with a middle-aged man sitting next to him. The man's face looked drawn and tired even after a night's rest. When Nickolai expressed care and concern, the man introduced himself as Yuri and said that he was returning to his home in the small town of Krasnodon. He worked in the city of Kharkov, but his wife and children lived in Krasnodon, tending to the gardens at the family dacha. It was difficult for the family to be apart all the time, but like most families in the Ukraine, it was the only way they could make ends meet financially.

Yuri had recently received a letter from home telling him that his wife was sick and that he'd better catch the next train to Krasnodon. "She has bleeding spells, usually from the nose," Yuri confided. "The doctors have done all they can, but it is not a good situation. One time last year she bled so much that she had to stay in bed for more than a week until she could get her strength back."

He paused and then continued, "Her condition is very serious again, but we don't know what's causing the bleeding or how to stop it. I'm afraid I'm going to lose her, and it scares me more than anything I've ever had to face in my life."

The man's voice grew somber. "It frightens her too," he added, and Nickolai could see fear clearly written on his face. "Death is a dark place—no one knows what happens to a person when they die."

Nickolai listened to the man and saw the desperate need in his eyes. He could tell that this man was in need of comfort. If Nickolai could give him even one ray of hope, he knew it would help.

And so Nickolai began to tell him stories about Jesus and the healing power that God can bring to a life. He explained to Yuri that he didn't need to worry about death, because the Creator of life had conquered death. Jesus, God's Son, had died for the sins of the world and then rose again from the dead. He is in heaven now and has the power to give the gift of eternal life to all who will accept it.

"Are you a priest?" Yuri suddenly asked. "You speak of God as though you know Him well, and you speak of the future as though you have already seen it."

Nickolai smiled warmly. "I'm a pastor," he admitted, "and I love God very much. As for the future, I have a wonderful book that tells me what to expect so that I can be ready for it when it comes."

"I wish it was possible for you to come to my village," Yuri said. "My wife would be so happy to meet you, I'm sure. Maybe you could even help her with her illness."

It was then that Nickolai shared with Yuri and the other passengers why he was on the train as a prisoner. He spoke about his churches and how much everyone loved Jesus. He spoke of his refusal to give the KGB the names of all his members.

No one said anything as Nickolai told his story. By the looks on their faces, he could tell that many of the passengers sympathized with him in his plight and the injustice of his sentence. Of course, no one dared express their true feelings for fear they might be accused of being sympathizers and end up being sent to a prison camp, as Nickolai was.

Yuri bowed his head dejectedly when he understood that Nickolai was not going to be able to go to his house and pray for his wife as he wished. However, what he said next surprised even Nickolai.

"Would you be willing to pray for my wife right now?" he asked.

Tears came to Nickolai's eyes as he witnessed the measure of faith Yuri had gained in the few minutes they had been talking.

The train car grew silent as Nickolai bowed his head and prayed for Yuri's sick wife and his children. It seemed that heaven had drawn very close, and the Spirit of God was hovering near.

When Nickolai finished praying, he noticed that a solemn look had come to the faces of many passengers on board. It was as if they understood the pain Yuri must be going through, but it also appeared as though Nickolai's prayer had touched them personally too.

When the train approached Krasnodon later that afternoon, Yuri thanked Nickolai for the prayer he had offered for his wife and family. And he expressed disappointment that he would never see Nickolai again.

"Take heart," Nickolai challenged Yuri. "We will meet each other again in heaven one day."

At this announcement several of the other passengers began to listen again, and some even came to sit close to where Nickolai and Yuri were talking.

"Because Jesus loves us so much, He left us some very special words. He doesn't want us to be discouraged while we wait for Him to come and take us home with Him.

"'Let not your heart be troubled,'" Nickolai began. "'You believe in God, believe also in Me. In My Father's house are many mansions; if it were not so, I would have told you. I go to prepare a place for you. And if I go and prepare a place for you, I will come again and receive you to Myself; that where I am, there you may be also' [John 14:1-3, NKJV]."

As the train pulled into the station, Nickolai prayed once again for Yuri's wife and children, and then for each person in that small circle on the train. Again Nickolai called upon the Master Physician to do for Yuri's wife what the doctors could not do, and again he sensed the Holy Spirit drawing near. It was an awesome and inspiring experience.

There were many tears when Nickolai finished his prayer, and many handshakes and hugs. It was as if Nickolai were a Christian apostle saying goodbye to his faithful members on one of his missionary trips around the world.

Chapter 4

During the next few days on the train Nickolai brought many more people to God. Several gave their hearts to Jesus and became Christians. Nickolai could not baptize them, but he encouraged them to find an Adventist pastor and ask that this be done for them.

After the train had been traveling eastward for several days, it finally neared the city of Omsk. Nickolai had heard that the prisoners would be transferred to another train when they arrived in Omsk, but that was as much information as he could get. No one had told him yet how far they had to go or how long it was going to take for the entire trip. Judging by the speed of the slowly moving train, Nickolai was guessing the trip would span at least 10 days.

Near sunset of the sixth day the train arrived in Omsk, a city known for its industry and oil production. Within the hour Nickolai and the other prisoners were transferred to a train heading north. By dark the train was lumbering across the plains, and Nickolai had settled in again for the remainder of the trip.

There were almost no passengers on this leg of the journey, because they were now riding on a freight train. In fact, other than the three prisoners and the two soldiers guarding them, the only other riders were the engineer, his furnace stoker, and a half dozen other workers who took up their positions near the end of the train.

Nickolai and his two fellow prisoners were confined in a mail car. Heavy manacles were now attached to their legs as well as their wrists so that they wouldn't be able to escape.

Nickolai smiled to himself as he stared out the window of the mail car and watched the landscape pass slowly by. Even if he could escape in these wastelands, where would he go?

As the train wound its way northward, the country became even more flat and littered with swampy muskegs. By now there were no trees in the desolate terrain.

For three long days the train crawled northward across mosquito-infested tundra and around small boggy lakes, but only once or twice did Nickolai see even a small village. He did catch a glimpse of reindeer herds, and now and then a few hunters following the herds. Nickolai wondered what it would be like to be on the open tundra. Would he be free to come and go as he pleased at the prison, or would he be locked up most of the time? It was at these moments that Nickolai found himself wondering about the decisions he had made during the past few weeks.

But then he remembered his commission. He was a pastor for God and an evangelist to the world. If God needed him in Kiev, then that is where he would preach for God. If God wanted him on a train bringing hope and the light of salvation to those who were discouraged, then that was his assignment. And if God wanted him to be in a prison camp in Siberia, then Siberia it was.

This kind of attitude bolstered Nickolai's faith and gave him courage to face whatever his imagination told him might be coming.

Somewhere in the wee morning hours of the third day, the engineer applied the brakes. As Nickolai stirred, the train slowed and came to a complete stop. The sun hadn't come up yet, but in the dusk of the northern twilight sky Nickolai could see the landscape clearly.

There was no train station, no village, and not even a sod hut or horse corral. In the glow of the moonlight, it was obvious there was nothing but the mosses, lichens, and scrubby tundra grasses of western Siberia. The landscape looked to be as desolate as any he had ever seen.

The air was damp and cool. The month of June had come, and with it the longer days of the north country. In fact, they were so far north that it never really got very dark at night. This time of year the sun set around 11:00 in the evening, dipping below the northern horizon, and then it came up again around 3:30 in the morning.

The three prisoners climbed out of the train, and with them the two soldiers guarding them. The soldiers pulled a half dozen packs from the mail car and gave them to the prisoners to carry.

As the train pulled away and disappeared to the north, all manacles and handcuffs were removed from the prisoners. Escaping was pointless. They were thousands of kilometers from home and hundreds of kilometers from the nearest train station or remote village.

Andryi, one of the prisoners, grew angry. "We have to walk!" he protested.

"That's right!" One of the guards waved his rifle in Andryi's face. "This is the end of the line for you! The rest of the way is on foot! And in case you haven't noticed," he snorted, "we guards are the ones who should be complaining, not you! We have to walk too, and we're not even criminals."

Andryi scowled at the two soldiers. "Well, how far is it?" he grumbled.

The other soldier stepped forward impatiently. "If we make good time, we can get to the camp by late tonight. And if I were you," he growled, "I wouldn't be thinking about taking too many rest stops. The tundra wolves out here are pretty big. It's June, so they might not be that hungry, but we don't want to take any chances. I've seen big ones take down a horse single-handedly."

"Now get going!" the first guard pointed his gun eastward. "The prison camp is that way! March!"

And with that the men walked off into the damp darkness. No flashlights, no torches—only the moon in the southern sky, the dim horizon to the north, and the stars still twinkling in the early-morning sky.

Chapter 5

The sun rose, and the men continued trudging across the Siberian landscape. The weather was pleasant enough, even with the sun shining down in its full strength. A slight breeze was blowing, but not enough to keep the mosquitoes, black flies, and no-see-ums from swarming around the men.

Nickolai and the other men had not taken baths for some time, and this ended up being a natural bug repellent against the insects. The flies and mosquitoes found the smell of sour sweat to be unpleasant and would alight for only a few seconds before moving on.

Unfortunately, this wasn't enough of a deterrent for the no-see-ums—they were the worst. They were so tiny that it was hard to see them, but they were there. They crawled into the men's eyes and ears and noses. They got into the men's hair and under the folds of their clothes. It seemed that no place was off-limits to the pesky little insects!

Eventually Nickolai smeared swamp mud on his face, neck, and hands to keep the bugs from biting. When the other men saw the way the mud protected Nickolai, they followed his example.

There was a faint trail across the tundra, which Nickolai felt must be the route to and from the prison camp. It wasn't an easy trail to walk, especially with all the bogs and muskegs everywhere. And skirting the spongy, swampy ground was tiring.

Not a soul appeared to be anywhere in the vicinity. As the day wore on without sign of human life, the strangest sort of panic began to creep over Nickolai. He felt as if he were walking to the edge of the earth's last wilderness, where absolute solitude existed. Surely human life could not exist in such a godforsaken place.

But then he remembered his resolve and his mission. Wherever he was headed, God needed him there. "This gospel of the kingdom shall be preached in all the world for a witness unto all nations; and then shall the end come" (Matthew 24:14). Those were words from one of Nickolai's favorite passages in Scripture, and they reminded him of his commitment to God. The idea calmed him a bit, and after a while he was able to regain his composure.

The men walked on and on long into the evening, but since the sun set so late this time of year, the way was clearly lit. And then, just as the sun dipped below the horizon, Nickolai caught sight of some buildings in the distance.

The men all quickened their pace. They had come so far. After 11 days of bread and water and handcuffs, their journey was finally over.

As they drew nearer the prison camp and the arctic summer twilight settled in with its deepening shadows, it was still light enough for Nickolai to take stock of the place.

It appeared that the camp had a kitchen and mess hall, and of course barracks for the prisoners to live in. There were other barns and sheds too, and a huge garden, maybe 2.5 acres (one hectare) in size. And sitting prominently in the middle of the camp was a building that looked like some kind of administrative headquarters.

But the thing that surprised Nickolai the most was the building materials. Most of the buildings were not made of wood—they were made of tundra sod. He had heard of such places where the soil, with its grassy roots, was cut out of the ground in blocks and stacked like bricks to make walls, but Nickolai had never actually seen it with his own eyes.

Most of the buildings were made of the sod, except the kitchen and administrative headquarters. What lumber was used in the camp must have been brought in by horse and wagon. There was no other way to get it here, Nickolai figured.

The building construction was quite simple, with tall stovepipes sticking through steep corrugated metal roofs designed to shed the heavy Siberian snows. Small doors and very few windows kept the openings in the buildings to a minimum. There was no doubt that this helped conserve the heat Nickolai knew they would need in the long, cold winters ahead.

In front of the building that looked like an administrative headquarters, a Soviet Union flag, with sickle and hammer stitched on it, flapped gently in the breeze. Nickolai sensed that even in this far-flung region, prisoners and guards alike had a sense of patriotism and national pride.

As the party of five arrived in camp, they caused quite a stir. The hour was late, but even so, prisoners and guards alike began to pour out of the barracks and other buildings. It was obvious that most of them had been roused from their sleep, but it didn't seem to matter.

This was the first contact anyone had had with the outside world in months. Everyone gathered around, curious to get a good look at the new prisoners. The soldiers had brought mail for the officers and guards on duty, and there were even a few select pieces for some of the prisoners. But mostly the inmates were just glad to see new faces and hear the latest news.

When all the excitement had died down, the prison warden emerged in a nightshirt. He looked the prisoners over with bloodshot eyes. It looked as if he had been drinking, but Nickolai wasn't surprised. Even in this place there had to be vodka.

There was vodka everywhere in Russia. The people used it to drink away their cares and troubles. They also used it for medicinal purposes, pouring it on cuts and wounds and infections. They even used it in their cars in the winter to keep the radiators and gasoline lines from freezing up.

And surely this prison warden used it to drink away the loneliness of the place. As Nickolai studied the face of the officer, he wondered where this man's family was. Did he have a wife? Did he have children? He looked to be in his early 40s. Was he considered a military officer?

The man looked as though he had let his appearance slide, but then again Nickolai had no idea what the standard was for officers in outposts like this one. Did anyone here really care how an officer looked? Nickolai guessed maybe not.

In the glow of twilight Nickolai could see that the warden's face of stubble already had a head start on the coming day. He had salt-and-pepper hair, and Nickolai had to smile. At least the man still had a full head of hair. Nickolai ran his hand over his own thinning scalp, reminding himself that he had less hair than the warden, though the warden looked to be older.

The warden greeted the prisoners gruffly, and then turned to go back into his own quarters. With a wave of his hand he sent them with a guard on a short tour of the camp.

Nickolai was surprised to discover that there were approximately 300 prisoners at the camp. The prison didn't appear to be big enough for those numbers, but judging by how cramped the bunks were in the barracks, he could believe it. Some 20 to 30 prisoners were crowded into a tiny room large enough for maybe 10 or 12. The only space Nickolai could call his own was his own bunk, which was little more than five feet in length. Rough-hewn boards formed the slats that made up each bunk frame and bed.

Nickolai frowned as he looked around and stared up at the tin roof of the barracks. Like it or not, this was going to be his new home. The sooner he got used to it, the better off he'd be.

Chapter 6

Near midnight Nickolai finally lay on his bunk, his feet hanging over the end of his bed. Unable to sleep, his mind raced at the strangeness of his new surroundings.

Again Nickolai was overcome with the remoteness of the place and the very simplicity of the camp. There were no prison walls, no barbed wire, and no guard towers. The guards didn't even carry guns. The very nature of such a prison defied all logic of what could and should be expected in the place.

There was obviously a chain of command from the top on down, as Nickolai was soon to learn. The warden oversaw the prison camp and reported to government officials higher up. Below him were the immediate officers in charge of the various functions of the camp. There were four junior officers. One was in charge of the guards and therefore, indirectly, the prisoners. A second was in charge of work detail units, and so it went.

And prisoners also answered to a pecking order of sorts among their own ranks. Those who had been at the prison camp the longest appeared to have seniority, but not always. If a man was big enough, strong enough, or intimidating enough, he could gain power and prestige among the prisoners.

But no matter the status of a prisoner, escape was out of the question. Nickolai was sure of that. Even in warm weather, to attempt such a thing seemed utterly foolish. Food, for starters, would be a problem, even if one could evade the guards who would no doubt be sent out as a posse. How much food would one have to carry in order to survive the march to civilization hundreds and hundreds of kilometers away?

Nickolai knew that wild creatures lived on the open plains, but he had seen very few of them. Reindeer herds ranged the open country, as he had observed while on the moving train, but Nickolai doubted that a lone man on foot with no weapons would be able to catch a reindeer, no matter how desperately he tried.

Of course there were the tundra wolves, arctic hares, snowy owls, and the many types of lemmings and mice he had been told lived in these parts. But all of them were considered unclean according to biblical standards. Nickolai knew that even if he could catch them, he would never be able to bring himself to eat that kind of meat, no matter how hungry he might be.

The idea of escape was ludicrous at best—and what was the point, anyway? They were all in this remote location together—warden, camp officers, guards, and prisoners. In order to survive the harshness of such an environment, each must do his part, even if there was a pecking order. They needed each other.

And that would have to be enough for now. It was all he could hope for. Here he was in this remote spot in the world, and there was no one he knew. No one to care what happened to him. There was no one it seemed to whom he could speak of loneliness. His fellow prisoners would have to be his confidants and cronies. They would have to be his friends.

But even so, as he tossed and turned, trying to fall asleep, his mind began to panic and scream out in protest, *How did I get myself into this?*

"Please, Lord!" he heard himself begging in whispered tones, "I pray that my time here will not be in vain. May You use me to speak to the other prisoners. May they see Jesus in me. If I can bring the gospel to them and let them see Jesus in me, that would be worth the pain and disappointment of having to be here.

"Let me be a witness to the guards, Lord. Though they mistreat me, let me bear their insults and abuse as You did— without complaining! Let them see that I am different, that the peace of heaven is on my face.

"And the warden? He's a Russian officer schooled in the ways of the military. In his world there is no God. Please, Lord, make him know beyond a shadow of a doubt that You exist. If I can be that person to help him see You and Your saving grace, I would be honored and willing to do that."

Nickolai began to feel the sweet peace of heaven settle over him. His prayer in the prison cell and on the train had been that God would be able to use him wherever he happened to be—wherever God could use his service.

"Lord, help me keep up my courage, and let me be faithful to You and the church I love," he breathed. "'Here I stand,'" he quoted the famous words from a book he loved, "'I can do no other. May God help me. Amen.'"

Somewhere in the twilight of the midnight sun Nickolai finally slept. And then it was morning.

Chapter 7

Nickolai sat bolt upright on the wooden boards of the bed where he lay sleeping. He tried to clear the fog from his tired mind to make sense of his surroundings. Where was he? What was he doing here?

"On your feet, men! We don't have all day to lie around spinning dreams! There's work to be done! On your feet!"

Nickolai heard a crash and then a groan just a few feet away. He turned on his bed to see a pile of boards from one of the bunks, and a man underneath them. Above him towered a guard, with shafts of dusty morning sunlight streaming through the open doorway behind him.

Now Nickolai remembered where he was.

The guard strode to where Nickolai was lying, but Nickolai scrambled to his feet and to attention before the guard could take a swipe at him too.

"That's better!" growled the guard in what Nickolai imagined must be a tone of satisfaction. "You've got 30 seconds to line up in front of the cabin! Better yet, let's see you make it in 20"

Without a second thought Nickolai dashed out into the early-morning sun now already well above the northeastern horizon. Even so, the hour was still early. Nickolai figured it couldn't be more than 5:00 or 5:30 in the morning.

He squinted at the brightness of the sun and wondered how the sun could rise so early this far north. But of course, with the tilt of the earth's axis during the summer months, places this far north had more daylight than cities farther south, such as Moscow or Kiev.

When the guard came out of the barracks, Nickolai was still trying to button his shirt and straighten his trousers. It was good that he had boots to wear and not shoes to lace up, or he wouldn't have made it out into the courtyard this fast with all his clothes on.

Nickolai glanced down at his appearance. It was true that his clothes weren't on completely straight, and his shirt wasn't buttoned up all the way, but he was relieved to know that he had somehow managed to straighten himself up in the few seconds the guard had allowed them.

Again Nickolai tried to shake the fog from his eyes and mind. There was no way to escape the reality of his surroundings. He was in a prison camp somewhere in Siberia at the end of a long train ride from the west.

And one thing was sure: If he was going to survive this place of desolation at the ends of the earth, he was going to have to learn to get up on time. Actually, getting up well before he was called would be better.

This was his first morning in camp, and it seemed that he was expected to know everything about the rules and regulations of the place. But Nickolai was quickly learning that one rule seemed to overshadow all others. "Never be late!"

He struggled to think positive thoughts as he stood at attention in the row of prisoners lined up in front of the barracks. The idea of having to do this every morning for the next five years, 10 years, or however long it took the KGB authorities to figure they had punished him enough, was almost more than he could bear.

"For being late you boys can skip breakfast this morning!" the guard barked. "That'll teach you to sleep in!"

No one moved.

"Well! What are you waiting for!" he growled. "You have your work details! Get to your assignments!

"You three!" he suddenly added, pointing at Nickolai and the other two new prisoners. "The warden wants to see you immediately!"

The three of them looked at one another with raised eyebrows, but when the guard turned and walked away, they shrugged and simply headed for the administrative building. Nickolai thought it strange that the men in his barracks had been caught sleeping in. Weren't they used to camp life? And weren't they used to getting up this early every morning, or was this just a show of force for Nickolai and the other new prisoners?

And why weren't he and the others being escorted to the warden's quarters? The whole thing seemed kind of strange, but then Nickolai remembered how informal the place was. People were just expected to go about their business and do their jobs, he guessed.

Nickolai was the last of the three to be called into the warden's office. As he stood at attention outside in the hallway, he wondered what went on in these kinds of prisons. What should he expect? Would he be interrogated again? Would he be mistreated because he was a Christian?

When Nickolai finally stood in the warden's office, he was surprised at how simple the place appeared. Though the warden was a colonel in the Russian army, there was almost nothing in his office to dress it up—a medium-sized oak desk, three chairs, a lone kerosene lamp, and a few books on a dusty bookshelf.

After studying an official letter that had been sent him via the mailbag on the train, the warden cleared his throat. "You had a run-in with the KGB."

Nickolai waited but said nothing, since the warden's statement was more commentary than anything.

"Nickolai Panchuk," the warden put the official letter back in a folder on his desk, "I've got no use for preachers! As far as I'm concerned, you preachers are all just a bunch of rebels!"

The warden brought his fist down on the desk with a bang. "You think you can change the world!" he growled. "Well, I've got news for you! The motherland is fine the way she is! The Union of Soviet Socialist Republics is the greatest nation the world has ever known! She doesn't need any help!"

The warden squinted at Nickolai through slit eyes. "Do you understand that, Panchuk?"

"Yes, sir!" Even though Nickolai was a Christian and didn't agree with the tactics the government used, he was still proud to be a citizen of the Soviet Union. It made his chest swell just to hear the national anthem or see athletes competing for the glory of the nation.

The officer leaned back in his chair. "I'll tell you what, Panchuk." He seemed to cool a bit. "Let's forget about what it was that got you here in the first place. If you follow my orders in this camp, I'll not give you any trouble. We'll let bygones be bygones. What do you say to that?"

The warden began sorting through some other papers on his desk.

Nickolai wondered whether the warden fully understood the charges being brought against him. He had to, didn't he? The man had Nickolai's file! Did he know about the secret churches? Would he be expecting Nickolai to give him the list of church members?

Of course, Nickolai knew he would never give such a list to the warden! Not even if the warden should beat him! Not even if the warden should kill him. But of course the warden didn't know that. Nickolai wondered if he should just bring up the subject and get it all out in the open now. On the other hand, maybe he should just let the warden figure it out for himself.

"I want to cooperate, sir!" Nickolai's face was stolid as he stood at attention and stared straight ahead.

The warden stood to his feet suddenly. "Good, Nickolai. I'm glad to hear that." A slight grin edged the corners of his mouth. "Now, I'm sending you to the wood shop. You'll be working with Vadeem, the camp carpenter. Lots of work to do around here," he announced.

"And remember, Panchuk," he added as he pointed the way for Nickolai, "follow orders, and you and I will get along just fine."

Chapter 8

Nickolai couldn't believe his ears. That was it? No interrogation? No grilling to get long-sought-after information from "the preacher"?

This was too good to be true. It couldn't be that easy, and Nickolai was sure there would be future confrontations.

As he turned to go, Nickolai suddenly remembered his biggest problem of all—the Sabbath. He would be required to work during Sabbath hours. That's what happened when you were a prisoner.

Nickolai wondered. Should he say something about it now or wait until Saturday, when the Sabbath would actually become an issue?

Nickolai knew he'd better take care of it immediately while he still had the courage and the warden's attention.

"Sir," Nickolai stopped and turned around. "There is one thing that may be a problem."

But already the warden had moved on to other things. "Remember, Panchuk. No problems. Simply obey orders, and you and I will get along fine."

And with that the warden waved him out the door.

Nickolai stood a few moments longer, wondering what he should do, but he realized there was no use pressing the issue now. The warden was in no mood to listen, and maybe it wasn't the right time for such a discussion anyway. God had His own timetable as to when these things should be taken care of, Nickolai mused. He knew he'd better let God work everything out as He saw best. *Help me know when that time is,* he silently prayed.

Nickolai went looking for Vadeem, the camp carpenter, and found him in the wood shop. Vadeem still had the pungent odor of garlic on his breath, and the smell of it made Nickolai ravenous. Garlic was one of his favorite foods, and knowing that he had been deprived of breakfast made it twice as hard to go to work and wait for the midday meal.

But Vadeem had plenty for Nickolai to do, and that made him almost forget the grumbling, growling feeling in his stomach. The mess hall needed more wooden benches made. Then there were the few boards in the floor of the administrative headquarters that needed to be replaced, and a door at the mess hall needed mending.

Lunch finally came. It was a simple one, but Nickolai didn't care. He was just glad to get something warm into his stomach. The cook had made borsch with beets, onions, and cabbage in it. It was the most heavenly food Nickolai could remember tasting. And the Russian black bread tasted like cake to Nickolai after his days on the train with so little to eat.

That afternoon Vadeem told Nickolai they needed to repair some of the large wooden water barrels sitting near the kitchen. Each barrel held about 50 gallons of water and was made with oak staves. Nickolai had to tip them on their side to roll them back to the wood shop, where Vadeem would be making the repairs.

On his trip back for the second barrel, Nickolai noticed that an oxcart had pulled up at the kitchen. The cart held two large wooden barrels filled with water hauled from a spring located more than a half mile (one kilometer) away. Oleg, the driver of the oxcart, was shouting at the ox, trying to get him to pull the cart forward a bit more so the water could be hauled inside the kitchen, but the ox wouldn't budge a step farther.

Maybe the ox was tired from hauling the water, and maybe he was just being plain stubborn. Or maybe he was weary of the treatment he had been receiving from the driver.

At any rate, it was obviously a showdown, and it seemed both the driver and ox were determined to win. When the driver pulled out his leather prod and began to whip the ox in the face, Nickolai sprang into action. He knew it probably wasn't wise to get involved since this was only his first day in camp, but he couldn't bear to see the animal being mistreated.

"Hold on!" he called to the driver. "It's obvious the ox is too stubborn for his own good! Why don't we try something else?"

Nickolai tried not to look at the driver. He was butting in where he might not be wanted, but he felt he had to try.

"What's his name?" Nickolai asked nonchalantly as he stepped up to the ox and gave the animal a pat on his thick, muscled neck.

"Maksim, I guess," the prisoner replied. "I never use that name, but I guess it's his name."

"Animals are like people," Nickolai said. "They like to be convinced to do something—not beaten into submission."

Nickolai patted the ox's neck again and leaned forward to whisper something into its ear. Then he took hold of a halter around the ox's neck and pulled forward as he continued talking to the ox.

The technique did the trick. In a matter of seconds the ox had pulled the cart a short distance forward so the driver could unload the barrels and put them on pallets outside the kitchen.

That night after the evening meal Nickolai went to the stables, where he found Maksim quietly munching on tundra marsh grass. Nickolai sat down beside the big animal and watched him eat. He felt sorry for him. In some ways he thought he understood how Maksim must feel. The ox's job was to work every day, day in and day out, week after week, with no break. That seemed to be his only purpose in life.

And he was a prisoner like Nickolai. He was not his own boss. He couldn't come and go as he pleased. His job was to haul water from the spring, and it probably would be until the day he died.

After that first evening visit with Maksim, Nickolai

stopped by the stables every night to bring the ox a little something from the kitchen. Sometimes it was a beet or a wedge of cabbage. Sometimes it was just a small carrot, but it was the talks he had with Maksim that helped Nickolai the most.

Nickolai was sure that he was getting much more from the visits than Maksim was, but the animal seemed to enjoy the company. The one-sided conversations helped Nickolai deal with the pain of being so far from home. When he felt he was going to panic from the loneliness that threatened to overwhelm him, old Maksim would look at him with his big brown eyes and just listen.

And so a relationship began to grow between Nickolai and Maksim. It was a wonderful tonic for Nickolai's spirit, and it helped him deal with the discouragement of those first few days in camp.

Chapter 9

As the week progressed, Nickolai knew the Sabbath problem wasn't going to go away. He was going to have to face it. Several times he wondered how he should break the news to the warden, but there seemed to be no good way to do it, and no good time, either. The warden kept to himself and didn't invite many visitors to his office. One thing was sure. He had Nickolai's file in his office, and sooner or later it would probably be used against him.

The Sabbath hadn't been a specific problem on Nickolai's record—the thing that had gotten him into trouble had been his unwillingness to cooperate with the KGB and give them a list of his church members. But would the Sabbath be a problem now? Nickolai could hardly imagine that it wouldn't, since the warden had reminded him that obeying the camp rules was extremely important. And Nickolai hadn't heard that there were any days off for rest or recreation.

As Thursday and then Friday came, Nickolai knew a showdown was imminent.

On Sabbath morning, long before the roosters were crowing over in the chicken coop, Nickolai was up, restless and waiting for the will of God to be revealed. "What is it You have in store for me?" Nickolai whispered as he knelt in the early-morning shadows of the sod barracks. "I know You want me to be Your witness, and I know I may have to suffer for Your sake, but how am I to know Your plans for me?"

But the voice of God was strangely silent, and Nickolai knew that this was one of those times he would simply have to wait for God to lead.

When he heard the other prisoners in his barracks begin to stir, he knew the time was fast approaching. And since God had not told him what to do, Nickolai made a decision—he would go out to roll call, but not to breakfast or his work assignment. After roll call he would return to the barracks to fast and pray. Come what may, this was his decision, and he would stick by it.

And that was it. It was as though God had been waiting for Nickolai to make a decision about the Sabbath and then act on it. It was this moment of decision that gave Nickolai the confidence he had been lacking all week. Suddenly he could see things clearly, as though a window of opportunity had opened.

He was standing on the threshold of another great moment in his life. He sensed that things were going to be very hard for him now that he had made this decision, but he wanted to go through with it anyway.

After roll call he did exactly as he had planned. He returned to the barracks, knelt down again on the hard dirt floor by his bunk, and began to pray. And every moment that passed took him closer to the inevitable confrontation he knew was coming.

But it didn't come as soon as he had expected, and he should have guessed as much. No one would know that he hadn't shown up for his work assignment except Vadeem, and the carpenter might simply think that Nickolai had been asked to work somewhere else for the day.

But finally the moment of truth arrived. About mid-morning Nickolai heard one of the guards outside talking to another prisoner.

"Where's Panchuk!" the gravelly voice demanded.

"I haven't seen him," came the reply.

It was almost noon before Nickolai was finally discovered in the barracks, and when he was, it seemed the whole world was caving in.

"What are you doing here?" the guard demanded. "Are you sick?"

Nickolai knew that if he said he was sick, they might let him off for the day, but that wouldn't fix the problem. The following week he would be in the barracks again, and the likelihood of his being sick two Sabbaths in a row would certainly be cause for suspicion. Nickolai knew he needed to deal with the Sabbath issue now. He needed to face this problem head-on no matter what the consequences. It was the only way.

"I'm not sick," Nickolai said plainly, getting to his feet.

"Then why are you in here!" the guard asked incredulously as though expecting some sort of ridiculous answer. And he got one.

"I can't work today because it's the seventh-day Sabbath of the Lord my God."

"The seventh-day what!" the guard yelled, standing stock-still.

"The seventh day is God's holy Sabbath, and I'm forbidden to work on it. The Bible is very—"

"The Bible!" Nickolai was cut short by the guard. It was obvious the guard hadn't seen this coming, and it gave Nickolai a chance to take the explanation a bit further.

"The Bible is God's Holy Word, and in it He tells me I should worship Him on the seventh-day Sabbath in honor of the world's creation." Nickolai would have liked to say more, but he knew the guard would never let him finish, and he was right.

"I don't know what you're talking about!" the guard interrupted again, finally getting his bearings. "It doesn't matter what day it is! We work every day around here! On your feet, Panchuk! I won't have any slackers in these barracks!"

But Nickolai made no move to go, and this infuriated the guard even more.

"I'll teach you to disobey orders!" he shouted again, his face turning purple with rage. He pulled a nightstick from his belt and began to beat Nickolai on the head and shoulders.

Nickolai didn't have time to do anything but cover his head with his hands and arms. It hurt, but he was able to deflect the worst blows of the beating.

"Now get to your work assignment!" the guard shouted. "Vadeem is looking for you!" Both Nickolai and the guard were breathing hard by now, but Nickolai still made no move to go.

"I'm sorry, but I can't work," Nickolai repeated the words quietly. "It's forbidden for me to work on God's holy day."

At this the guard let loose with a steady stream of curses and began to beat Nickolai mercilessly with his fists. Then he grabbed Nickolai by his shirt collar and dragged him out the door into the barracks courtyard.

By now the commotion was so great that other prisoners were looking toward them to see what the noise was all about.

"We'll see about this seven day holy Sabbath of yours!" he shouted uncontrollably. "We'll just take you to the warden and see what he says about all this! He'll know what to do with the likes of you!"

Chapter 10

Moments later Nickolai was in front of the warden's office. Although he was still standing, he was a sorry sight. His face was beginning to swell from the beating he had received to his head. One eye was turning black, his shirt was almost ripped off, and his hair was all covered with dirt and straw.

"What's the meaning of this!" the warden demanded, coming out of his office. When he saw Nickolai, he began to walk round and round him.

"He insists that he can't work today because it's some kind of holy day!" snapped the guard.

"A holy day, is it? Well now, Yuri," the warden turned to the guard. "I see that you tried to enlighten this man on the ways of our camp. You are to be commended."

By now Nickolai could hardly see through the eye that was swelling shut. He was indeed suffering for the decision he had made to keep God's Sabbath holy, but it didn't matter. This was a small price to pay compared to the suffering that Jesus had endured for Nickolai. What harm could it do to suffer a little for Him?

The warden turned back to Nickolai. "What have you got to say for yourself, troublemaker?"

"It's true," Nickolai admitted. Although he could not see clearly, he stared straight ahead again, not looking directly at the warden.

"Well, I hope you've learned your lesson." His voice was as smooth as syrup as he came to stand in front of Nickolai, but beneath it all Nickolai sensed the man could be cruel.

"Are you ready to go back to work?" He stood toe to toe with the prisoner, his nose barely inches from Nickolai's face.

"It's God's holy day. I cannot work on the seventh-day Sabbath."

The warden's eyes grew steely cold. "You can't work?" he asked plainly, his voice strangely calm, but Nickolai could tell there was disdain beneath the calm exterior, and he sensed that the worst was yet to come.

"Not on God's holy day."

"Is that your final answer?"

"Yes, sir."

"The consequences will be severe." The warden's voice was still even, but the tension was building.

"It's my decision, sir. I'm willing to take the punishment."

"And you will." The warden turned to Yuri with ice in his voice, and he had a cold gleam in his eye. "Go get my whip from my office. Strip the preacher to the waist and tie him to the flagpole. We'll see how strong this boy is."

Nickolai was brave, but he found it difficult to keep from crying out in pain. The warden did indeed make a spectacle of Nickolai as he beat him mercilessly with the whip. Finally Nickolai slumped to the ground unconscious, and it was only then that the warden stopped long enough to catch his breath.

He wiped the sweat from his forehead and handed the whip to Yuri. "Cut him loose. When he comes to, he can find his own way back to the barracks."

And with that the warden went back inside his office. Yuri watched him go, not surprised, but a bit solemn at this display of the warden's fury. It had been a long time since he had seen the warden beat a prisoner like this, and it was a bit disturbing for him to see the warden enjoy it so.

He himself had beaten Nickolai just minutes before, but now he realized what anger could do to someone if unchecked. It was a rather strange mixture of feelings, and he was hard-pressed to explain the anger that he and the warden felt toward these prisoners.

How long Nickolai lay on the ground he didn't know. The sun was low in the sky when he finally came to, and he could hardly move. The blood had dried on his back, but the flies were having a feast. After a bit he finally managed to stand and slowly stagger back to the barracks. When he got there, he collapsed on his bunk and fell into an exhausted sleep.

The next day his back felt like chopped meat, but he managed to get to his feet. He was able to wash the blood from his face, but he couldn't reach his back. His shirt covered the lacerations on his back, but his face was black and blue for all to see.

And not surprisingly, the other prisoners avoided him. It was too risky to do otherwise. After all, who would want to befriend a foolish preacher who would rather be horse-whipped than give in to the warden's demands? Any one of them might be considered a sympathizer if they were caught talking to Nickolai.

During the next few days Nickolai grew stronger. The wounds healed slowly, but his courage grew with each day. He had passed the test. He had been strong for Jesus. He had not given in even though he knew he would suffer for it.

As the days passed, the other prisoners still avoided him, but he thought he saw faint looks of admiration directed toward him. Tuesday came and went, and then Wednesday and Thursday. Nickolai began to think of the coming Sabbath. What would be his fate? Would the warden respect him for his stand on the Sabbath? Would he grant him the privilege to rest as he had asked?

Or would it be just the opposite? Would he get another beating for his decision to honor the Sabbath?

Unfortunately, Nickolai couldn't see that worse was still to come, and it was just as well. He needed to grow a bit stronger before Satan's tide of evil would again hit him with all its force.

Chapter 11

All week Nickolai worried about what would happen on Sabbath morning. He knew he shouldn't worry, but he dreaded what might be coming next. He thought he would be willing to take more of the same treatment he had already received, but his wounds hadn't healed yet from the warden's initial horsewhipping. If he was whipped again, the wounds would just open up again, and he could only imagine what the pain would be like then.

By Friday night, though, his faith was strong, and he was determined to stand for God and face whatever was in store for him tomorrow. If God would give him the courage and the strength to go on, Nickolai was determined to be faithful to God no matter what happened.

Sabbath dawned cool and clear. Nickolai didn't know how early he had awakened. He didn't have a watch, but he could tell by the snoring in the barracks that it was early— well before the usual time to rise.

Because of the lacerations and bruises on his back, Nickolai had been sleeping on his stomach, but now he rolled out of bed and onto his knees.

"Please, Lord!" he prayed. "Let me be worthy of the persecution that might come my way today. I know it's a small thing compared to what You did for me, but I'll gladly do it."

How long he stayed on his knees he couldn't say, but suddenly Yuri's gravelly voice was waking everyone in the barracks as though it were the judgment day.

"On your feet, men! Out of those beds!"

Yuri gave a few of the beds a jarring kick, sending prisoners flying out of them in a hurry.

Nickolai jumped to his feet too, but not before Yuri noticed him.

"Well, now, Panchuk! It's nice to see that we're not going to have any foolishness this morning. I can see that you've come to your senses!"

Nickolai smiled weakly, but said nothing. He knew trouble was already on its way, but what should he say? No matter what he said, the whole thing was going to blow up in his face.

All the soldiers filed out into the morning sunshine and waited for their orders after roll call. The officer in charge of camp maintenance and repairs read down through a list of the tasks for the day. Several of the prisoners in Nickolai's barracks were to work with a crew that would be helping to butcher some reindeer meat brought in the day before. The dozen or so animals had somehow split off from a larger herd and migrated west toward the camp, where the guards spotted them though field glasses.

Other prisoners were sent to cut new sod to build yet another barracks that was soon to go up. It had been rumored that another batch of prisoners would be coming in the next month, and the current barracks were already bursting to overflowing.

"And Panchuk?" Yuri looked straight at Nickolai. "You are to report to Vadeem immediately after breakfast. He needs to do some roof repairs on the mess hall."

Nickolai looked straight ahead. The moment he feared most had arrived, and of course he wasn't surprised. Would the confrontations and beatings start all over again?

"Well! What are you waiting for?" Yuri demanded as Nickolai looked straight ahead and didn't offer to move.

He opened his mouth to speak, but then closed it again. What was the use? They were going to mistreat him anyway, no matter what he said.

But then he remembered his promise to God that he would speak for the Lord wherever he was sent, or in whatever he was asked to do.

Nickolai took a deep breath. "I can't work today because it's the seventh-day Sabbath of the Lord my God."

The guard's face took on a shocked look of exasperation, but then turned to annoyance.

"Preacher man! You have got to be kidding!" he blurted. The other prisoners stared at Nickolai and shook their heads silently.

Yuri finally overcame his silence and snorted, "So you've decided to be stupid again, have you? Well, we'll see about that!"

He grabbed Nickolai by the arm and marched him off to the warden's office, and then left him standing in the hallway just outside the imposing doorway.

Nickolai finally dredged up enough courage to knock on the door. Maybe the warden wasn't in, Nickolai hoped. Maybe he was busy doing something more important.

But soon the door opened, and when the warden saw Nickolai, a look of disbelief came across his face.

"What do you want, Panchuk?" he shook his head pathetically. "Don't tell me! You've decided to be stubborn again!" The warden came right to the point. It was as if he had somehow known all along that Nickolai would refuse to work again come Saturday but had never really allowed himself to imagine it.

Nickolai opened his mouth to speak again, but the warden cut him off.

"All right! If that's the way you want it! Come with me!" he stood to his feet, stepped through the open doorway, and then down the short hallway.

Nickolai stood rooted to the spot as he watched the warden go.

Chapter 12

The warden turned impatiently. "Panchuk! Get a move on it!" he snapped. "Try to keep up!"

Nickolai hurriedly fell in step behind the warden as they exited the building. What would happen next? Was he going to be given a pass from work for the day? Was he going to be allowed to rest and worship according to his convictions?

The warden walked to one of the sod sheds and opened the door. It was the stables where old Maksim was kept, and it smelled of it. There were no windows in the building, so the inside appeared dark and foreboding. This didn't look good. Undoubtedly for Nickolai things were going from bad to worse. Was he going to be beaten again? Was he going to be tortured? Nickolai cringed. Was he going to be executed?

Suddenly Nickolai began to panic. During his early-morning prayers his imagination had run wild with all kinds of abuse that he knew they could heap on him, but he hadn't really thought of death. Not really. Death had always seemed so remote out here, where there was so much work to be done. In a camp like this, where the prisoners did all the work, executing a prisoner seemed pointless.

Nickolai knew this kind of logic bordered on insanity. He had to get a grip. He watched as the warden walked to a corner of the dark stables where a wooden box sat. It didn't look to be more than a yard (one meter) long or high, and possibly a half yard (half meter) wide.

Nickolai's heart began to hammer wildly in his chest like a caged animal. Was this the end? He tried to calm his racing heart, but there was no time to think. No time to collect his wits.

Then he remembered his prayer that morning and his promise to God. He had pledged himself to suffer anything for God, so why not now? Why not this? Whatever the warden had in store for him, it couldn't be worse than what Jesus had suffered for him.

The warden lifted the top off the wooden box. Even in the dim shadows of the sod stable, Nickolai could see that the box was empty.

"Get in," the warden ordered.

"Get in?" Nickolai echoed.

The warden didn't reply, but motioned with his head toward the crate.

"The box? I'm supposed to get in the box?"

"Do I need to spell it out for you! Yes, you're supposed to get in the box!" The stables echoed the stillness of the moment. "Now get moving! I don't have all day!"

Nickolai took one last look at the warden and then stepped toward the box. He lifted a leg and got inside—it was smaller than it looked.

"Sit down!" the warden ordered.

As the lid slammed down over him, a shower of dust choked Nickolai, making him wheeze.

"Hope you like your new home," the warden called as he turned to go.

The wooden slats of the box were thick, so it looked like it would be next to impossible to break his way out. And besides, what would it accomplish? The warden would just build a stronger box to hold him.

He had heard of boxes like this one being used to keep prisoners locked up, but this box had so many cobwebs it didn't look as though it had been used in years. Maybe the box was used for the hardest of criminals. Maybe the other prisoners just behaved themselves and didn't get themselves into predicaments, as Nickolai had.

The light from the open doorway told Nickolai that there were cracks in the sides of the box. He would have no problem breathing, but keeping his legs from cramping up was going to be a trick. He couldn't stand up and he couldn't lie down, so he couldn't stretch his legs out.

Nickolai wanted to give up in despair, but he knew that wasn't an option. Not when he had promised himself that he was going to be true to God and be His steadfast witness. Suffering was the least of his worries. Failing to trust in God was a bigger concern right now.

Nickolai closed his eyes and leaned against the inside wall of the box. He knew this was not going to be a pleasant experience. In fact, it promised to be downright excruciating. How long would they wait before they let him out of the box? Days? Weeks? Would they bring him food? Would they give him water? Would they let him out to go to the bathroom?

"Please, Lord, don't let me become discouraged," he prayed. "Don't let my faith in You fail."

As the hours slowly passed, the light in the stable doorway changed direction and then finally began to grow dim. About that time Oleg, the oxcart driver, came into the shed leading old Maksim. Oleg gave the animal food and water, and then left. Nickolai thought Oleg might at least have offered him some water, but then realized that he should have asked. What had he been thinking? Oleg probably didn't even know that Nickolai was locked in the box in the shed.

"Hello, Maksim," Nickolai finally called to the ox, trying to cheer himself up. "I hope your day was better than mine."

As Nickolai sat in the box, he could hear the old ox munching the sedge grass in his manger. He thought about how hard the ox had to work as a beast of burden every day, and he even found himself feeling sorry for the ox.

Right now, though, he thought he would gladly change places with the ox. Even if he had to pull an oxcart loaded with water barrels all the way from the spring, it would be better than sitting in this box all day.

Chapter 13

As darkness settled in, the mosquitoes came in droves. They bit at Nickolai's neck and face until he finally stopped swatting at them and gave up the fight. Right now the worst thing about being in the box was the mosquitoes, but he sensed that not being able to stretch his legs was going to be a nightmare.

Eventually he dozed. He didn't sleep well with the mosquitoes everywhere, but he did doze off.

Somewhere in the night he awoke and couldn't go back to sleep. His mouth was dry—he hadn't had water all day, and he wondered when they would bring him some. Had the guards forgotten that he would need water? He was hungry too—who could say when he'd get a chance to eat again?

But it was the circulation in his legs that worried him most. By now his ankles and feet felt numb with stiffness from his legs being bent up so close to his body. He tried to get the blood flowing in his legs, but it was difficult because the box was so small. There just wasn't room enough to stretch out inside the box.

At times like this he wished that he were a smaller man. If he hadn't felt so miserable, Nickolai might have smiled at such a thought. Being a bit shorter would have allowed him some room to get more exercise in the small box.

But there was to be no relief for the numbness that kept coming back to his lower legs. Finally he began to pray again, as he had done a dozen times since being locked up in the box. It was the only thing that made him feel better. That and the verses of Scripture he quoted to bring himself comfort.

When the sun finally came up, he felt as if it had been the longest night of his life. When Oleg came to get Maksim, Nickolai asked him if he could have some water. Oleg was startled to hear Nickolai's voice from the box.

"What are you doing in there?" Oleg asked, peering into the shadows. "Did the warden put you in that box?"

"He did." Nickolai felt a bit embarrassed, but he decided he wouldn't try to hide the reason. "I refused to work yesterday on the Sabbath, so he put me in here to punish me."

"I heard that you had been punished, but I didn't know where you were." Oleg shook his head. "I'd better not give you water. They might not like it."

"Can you ask one of the guards to bring me some, then? I think they may have forgotten me here. No one's been out here except you since they put me in here yesterday."

"I'll see what I can do."

But the guards never came with any water, or any food, either. All day Nickolai worked to keep his legs moving, and all day he prayed. By now he knew that his time in the box was going to be a long ordeal. He didn't quite know what to expect because the warden didn't say how long he would have to stay in the box.

Every time he heard footsteps he thought it might be someone coming to bring him water or food, or to let him out of the box to stretch.

Sometime late that afternoon a guard did come into the shed to give Nickolai a can of water, but no food. The water felt cool and wet to his parched lips and throat—and yet at thirsty as he was, Nickolai wisely decided to save some of the water for later.

Oleg came in with Maksim later that night, and again Nickolai was glad to have the company of someone to talk to, even if it was just an ox.

The night passed in extreme discomfort. The mosquitoes made it almost impossible for him to sleep, and of course the numbing pain in his legs was the worst of all.

Nickolai wished that he could get out of the box to use a bathroom, but no one let him out, so the box soon developed an unpleasant odor. Unfortunately there was nothing Nickolai could do about it.

The hours slowly passed, with Oleg and Maksim leaving early the next morning and then returning again sometime before dark. A guard came with water again, but still no food. Night came once more, and by now it took all Nickolai's faith and energy just to pray. Did anyone care about him? Was there no value to his life?

And what about God? Did He care that Nickolai was suffering? Nickolai knew the answer to that last question, but he was really feeling sorry for himself by now. God could help relieve his suffering, but He was not choosing to do so right now. There had to be a good reason, of course.

Through all those long days filled with pain and loneliness and frustrated faith, Nickolai held to the Scripture promises he had always believed in. Satan wanted to make him suffer, but God loved him more than he could possibly imagine. There was a battle going on between good and evil, a war zone in which Nickolai was suffering as much pain and persecution as Satan could muster.

Jesus suffered for me with pain that was indescribable. Why should my experience for Him be any different? Nickolai tried to bolster his courage with these thoughts, but it was difficult.

As with the story of Job, Nickolai knew that some pain and heartache could not be explained except in light of the invisible war going on in the supernatural world. When he thought about it in this way, it seemed to help more than anything else.

One thing was for sure: While Nickolai was locked up in the box, he could have his Sabbath rest. It wasn't exactly the place he would have chosen to spend the Lord's day, but at least he didn't have to work. No matter how Nickolai looked at it, he had to admit it was a blessing in disguise.

Chapter 14

The weekend passed, and Monday came and went. By now the thought of food had almost gone from Nickolai's mind. He had not eaten in nine days. It was as if his body had slipped into another world that no longer required him to eat. Of course, he was getting weaker every day, but being in the box didn't require much movement, so it also required very little energy.

However, there was a dull throbbing pain in his legs, and that scared Nickolai more than anything. During the first few days in the box, the pain had been pretty bad whenever he moved his legs. Now he couldn't make them move of their own accord. It was as if they were logs of wood attached to his body at the hips—he couldn't really feel them much anymore. He worked on them all the time, using his arms to move them every day, many times a day.

By Tuesday of the second week the box smelled rank beyond description, and the flies were everywhere. It was a living nightmare. Nickolai no longer worried about the warden. He no longer worried about food or water. He just prayed that God would give him the strength to make it through another day.

Around noon on the tenth day, Nickolai heard footsteps. He peered through the slats and saw the warden standing in the doorway. Yuri, the barracks guard, was with him.

"Open the box," the warden said. That was all. It was as if this were a mere formality in the life and duties of a warden at the prison camp.

To Nickolai it had been the worst experience of his life.

Yuri opened the lid of the box. "Oh!" he sputtered as he held his hand over his mouth. "You smell putrid! Get out of the box!" he ordered, shaking his head in disgust. "You're free to go!"

But Nickolai couldn't stand.

Yuri reached down and lifted Nickolai out of the box. When he saw that Nickolai couldn't walk, his face grew serious, and a look of compassion filled his eyes. He helped Nickolai to a bed of straw and let him lie down.

"I'll be all right," Nickolai assured him with a weak smile. Right now he just wanted to be alone so that he could scream out in pain if he needed to. For 10 days he hadn't been able to move his legs properly, and now the pain of moving them was almost as excruciating as having his legs cramped up in the box.

All the rest of that day Nickolai lay on the straw, trying to gain his strength and flex his legs so that he could walk on them. Yuri brought him a tin plate of borsch at the supper hour, and Nickolai managed to eat a few bites—he wasn't foolish enough to eat it all. After being deprived of food for so long, he knew his stomach would never be able to handle that much food.

Before dusk Oleg and Maksim came in from their long day of hauling water. Once again Nickolai felt a sense of kinship with the ox and was glad for his company. As the night settled in, Nickolai didn't even try to go to the barracks, but stayed in the stables with Maksim instead. In fact, when the ox finally lay down in the straw, Nickolai crawled over to warm himself by the animal's big body.

Nickolai then dropped into a sleep so deep that he never even noticed the mosquitoes swarming around him. Surprisingly, they didn't bother him much that night. Maybe it was the fact that he smelled so bad.

The next morning Nickolai felt much better. He could stand some and even walk a bit. The guard brought more food for him—a bowl of borsch and some Russian black bread. Again Nickolai was careful about the amount he ate, but he did manage to eat more than he had the day before.

He cleaned up and then went back to work with Vadeem, though he found he couldn't lift much of anything. He didn't have any strength in his arms or legs, and he tired easily.

"Not surprising!" Vadeem looked at Nickolai as if the preacher man were crazy. "You must have a death wish!" he chided. "Whatever would possess you to put yourself through 10 days of torture in that box!"

Nickolai tried to explain about his love for God, and God's love for the human race. He tried to explain about his sacred devotion to the Sabbath. But Vadeem just shook his head in disbelief and muttered to himself under his breath.

By Thursday morning Nickolai could get around pretty well, though he did have a limp in his stride. Friday arrived, and for the first time since he had been pulled from the box, Nickolai allowed himself to think about what the next morning might bring. To him Sabbath was a very special day, whether he was in a church or a lonely prison camp. However, Sabbath also meant that he was going to have to face the warden again. What would the high-ranking officer do this time?

The first time Nickolai had been severely beaten by both Yuri and the warden. The second Sabbath they had locked him up in a box for 10 days. On the third time around would they finally give up, or would the persecutions continue?

Nickolai wondered how much worse things could get. He was sure that there would be another confrontation with the warden, and he dreaded it, but he also knew that he had to remain faithful to God no matter what. He couldn't give up now. The Sabbath was his special blessing from God. With all his heart he wanted to honor the sacred day and the Creator God who had designed it.

Chapter 15

The night was moving slowly into the first shades of dawn when Nickolai suddenly awoke. What it was that had awakened him he couldn't say. It wasn't the noise of anyone else in the barracks. They were all still sleeping, though Nickolai was sure their laborious snoring could have kept him awake all night if he hadn't been so tired.

It wasn't the sound of birds. There were very few songbirds out here on the Siberian steppes.

Nickolai wondered if it was his mind working overtime that had awakened him with a start. And what could he expect? The ordeal through which he had been during the past two weeks had been horrible! Dreadfully uncomfortable!

And what about the next go-round with the warden? Nickolai feared it would be as bad as the times before. Maybe worse.

But he was calm (surprisingly so), and it felt strange. To be sure, he didn't relish the idea of spending more time in a box, if that's what the warden had in store for him, but for some reason Nickolai didn't feel as though he needed to escape the approaching hardship the warden might bring. In fact, he felt very little anxiety over it.

So why couldn't he sleep? Maybe he just needed more strength, the kind of strength he could get only through prayer.

Nickolai slipped out of bed and onto his knees to pray to his heavenly Father. It was wonderful to be able to call on the one who could give him help in time of need—wonderful to feel the presence of the Holy Spirit kneeling with him on the hard dirt floor beside that narrow bunk.

The longer he prayed, the more sure he was that he was going to have to suffer more. He would not be delivered from trouble. He would not be spared humiliation and pain. That's not the way it had usually worked for Nickolai, and he was OK with that right now. His faith might falter when he was tired, or lonely, or weak, but this morning in the cool dawn of the Siberian summer everything was going to be all right.

All too soon the sun rose and the 5:00 wake-up call came from the guards. The prisoners in the barracks slowly stirred and then rolled out of bed to avoid having the guards come in and flush them out.

For Nickolai another Sabbath day had dawned, and again he found himself at attention, standing in front of the bunkhouse. Again Yuri dismissed the men after roll call, but this time he kept his eye on Nickolai.

Nickolai knew it was pointless to prolong the agony of the moment. He didn't make a move, and of course Yuri noticed it. He came to where Nickolai was standing and stood with his big feet planted wide in front of the prisoner.

"Please don't tell me that you're going to refuse to work again!" he demanded in exasperation. "Because if it's true, I think I've probably met the dumbest man alive!"

Yuri continued to stare at Nickolai with something akin to awe on his face. He tried to hide it, but it remained there long enough to make them both uncomfortable.

And then the guard appeared to regain his composure as he seemed to brush the feeling off. "Forget it!" he half shouted. "Just get over to the warden's office right now!"

Nickolai knew Yuri was angry, and really, he had a right to be. What did he know of Nickolai or his God? What did he know of the love of a Creator for His children, and the devotion Nickolai felt for this God who had come to die for humanity? All Yuri knew was that this stubborn Christian pastor was making trouble and upsetting the routine of the camp.

Within seconds Nickolai had crossed the compound and was waiting in the doorway of the warden's office.

"What are you doing here, Panchuk?" The warden's eyes narrowed with surprise and skepticism and anger all in the same moment.

But Nickolai said nothing. He just stood at attention, his eyes focused forward. What could he say?

"I asked you a question, preacher man!"

Nickolai knew he dared not wait to answer the irate warden. But how could he make the warden understand why he wanted to honor the seventh day of the week? The warden was the product of a society that taught that there was no such thing as a loving personal God. He had been working in the military for decades and was indoctrinated with the concept that the only real answer to life was military force.

"I can't work today, sir," Nickolai began. "I can't dishonor God's holy Sabbath day."

The warden's face contorted with rage. He ground his teeth together and then brought a fist down on his desk.

"You're impossible, Panchuk! I have never in all my days met a man with your stubborn stupidity!" He rose to his feet and pushed Nickolai back out through the open doorway!

"Guard!" he shouted, looking down the hallway. "Get this man out of my office and take him back to the box!" The sound of running footsteps could be heard, and then Yuri was there, a look of disbelief on his face.

"Take Panchuk back to the box, Yuri. He likes it so much he wants to spend another 10 days there."

Yuri hung his head and then finally motioned for Nickolai to follow him to the stable. When they arrived at the box, he lifted the lid and motioned with his head for Nickolai to get in.

When the lid dropped down on Nickolai and the dust had settled, the "preacher man" had time to think about his decision.

He wasn't sorry. He had no regrets. He knew being locked in the box was going to be uncomfortable and excruciating, but he wasn't worried. For some strange reason he felt no anxiety or fear or dread of the next 10 days to come. It was all so bizarre; he couldn't explain it.

Some days he knew he was going to feel abandoned and alone, no doubt, but right here and now he was determined that he wouldn't lay the blame on God. It wasn't the Lord's fault that he was in this tiny prison of a box. It was the devil's fault—and the warden's, of course.

Chapter 16

Nickolai knew Satan was angry with him for his faithfulness under persecution and his desire to keep the Sabbath. He was angry with Nickolai for all he had done as a pastor to help spread the gospel. The evil one was frustrated with the way the church had been growing under Nickolai's leadership in Kiev and the surrounding towns of the Ukraine. Could anyone be surprised that Satan would do everything in his power to stop the work?

It was Satan who had incited the KGB to persecute Nickolai when he lived in Kiev. Satan had sent Nickolai to the Siberian tundra as a prisoner to be isolated for a very long time—the rest of his life, maybe. And now he was making life even harder for Nickolai by imprisoning him in a small box in which there wasn't even room enough for him to stretch his legs.

But it didn't matter. None of it mattered just now. Nickolai would serve his time in the box for the sake of the gospel. How many more times he was going to have to do this was anybody's guess. He hoped this would be his last, but Nickolai knew he was only fooling himself if he really believed that. The warden was angry and offended that nothing he did or said had worked to change Nickolai's mind and make him obey orders. He despised Nickolai's stubbornness, and Nickolai was going to have to pay the price for it.

However, if Nickolai was going to be stubborn about something, he wanted to be stubborn for the gospel of Jesus. He determined in his mind that he would outlast the best and the worst of what the warden could give him. And he would do it gladly.

As morning turned into afternoon and afternoon into early evening, Nickolai again consoled himself by praying and quoting Scripture. As the darkness of night descended upon the stable, Nickolai could feel the stiffness slowly but surely returning to his joints. He tried to keep his knees moving. He also decided to sing to lift his spirits. He didn't have much of a singing voice, but the words to a familiar hymn came to mind.

"'Under His wings I am safely abiding, though the night deepens and tempests are wild.'" The words were unsteady at first, but then Nickolai's voice grew stronger. "'Still I can trust Him; I know He will keep me; He has redeemed me, and I am His child.'" Nickolai's voice swelled even fuller on the chorus line.

"'Under His wings, under His wings, who from His love can sever? Under His wings my soul shall abide, safely abide forever.'"

The words worked like a tonic, and Nickolai realized that they were the magic he needed to keep his spirits up. In fact, all through that first night when he awoke to try to bend his stiffening knees, he would hum a few lines of the hymn. "'Under His wings, under His wings . . .'" And then he would doze off into a surprisingly restful sleep.

Of course, when he awakened the next morning it took him some time before he could get the circulation going in his legs again.

All that day and the following night he remembered his promise to himself and to God. Over and over he reminded himself that he was determined to be true to his beliefs. He would endure the discomfort of persecution for Jesus' sake, no matter what the price. He would manage the pain by praying and quoting Bible promises and singing hymns whenever he needed a spiritual boost.

The pain grew unbearable after only two days, but Nickolai's courage remained strong. He spent his time recounting the blessings God had given him and the good memories he had of his family and church back home.

The routine was the same. In the morning Nickolai would watch through the cracks of the box as Oleg came to take Maksim to work for the day. At night he would watch them return, tired after their many trips to the spring. Nickolai grew accustomed to the sound of the ox munching the sedge grass and his even breathing when he slept. It was a comfort to have another living creature near him—one that perhaps understood what it was like to be a prisoner against his will.

One thing was different this time around: Yuri made it a habit to bring Nickolai a can of water and a chunk of Russian black bread once a day. That was it, but it was better than nothing, and Nickolai was pretty sure that the bread was being brought in secret. He had detected a note of sympathy on Yuri's part, but he was sure the guard would never admit it.

If the warden shared any of Yuri's sentiments, he hid them well. Whatever scars there were that made the warden who he was ran deep, and Nickolai felt bad for the man.

About noon on the tenth day the lid to the box opened again. The fresh air and light were a shock to him, and again it was the face of the guard he saw first.

Yuri held a handkerchief over his nose and mouth as he shook his head disgustedly. "I don't understand you, preacher man," he said in a muffled tone, "and I probably never will!"

Again Yuri left Nickolai lying on the floor of the stable. Again Nickolai half crawled, half clawed his way to a pile of straw in the corner. The painful relief of being able to stretch his legs was excruciating, but Nickolai understood the pain this time around. He was getting used to the feeling of the box. He was ahead of the game this time.

Near dark Oleg returned to the stable with Maksim. When he had unhitched old Maksim, the ox came into the stable of his own accord. After all, it was his home. He paused as he walked past Nickolai and sniffed the smelly creature lying in the bed of straw.

Nickolai watched the ox eat his supper and then lie down in the soft straw beside him. Several times Nickolai thought he might attempt to crawl back to the barracks, but every time he tried to get to his knees, he would slump back onto the straw in pain. He was just too weak even to make it to the stable door, let alone all the way to the barracks.

But it didn't matter to Nickolai. He had nothing to lose one way or the other. In fact, sleeping next to Maksim's warm body was an advantage during the cooler nights.

As Nickolai dozed into a sleep of total exhaustion, he once again feebly hummed the familiar words, "safely abide forever."

Chapter 17

The next day Nickolai managed to get to his feet and limp back to the barracks. He couldn't go to the mess hall to eat, but Yuri brought him some borsch and Russian black bread.

Nickolai tried to thank the guard, but Yuri waved off the gesture as though he didn't want to hear it.

By Wednesday afternoon Nickolai thought he could probably work some if he didn't have to lift anything heavy or walk too much. No one was following him around to see that he worked, but he felt that it would be some kind of statement to the warden if he could get in a few hours of work before sunset Wednesday.

The week was half over, and Sabbath was looming on his weekly horizon. It would come, and when it did he had a feeling that the warden would put him back in the box. It was a battle of wills now between him and the warden. It appeared that the warden wanted to win this standoff at all costs, and if he couldn't, he was certainly going to make it a painful experience for Nickolai.

But pain or not, Nickolai also wanted to win this war that had now become one of government force versus allegiance to God.

Nickolai did work some on Wednesday, and then a full day on Thursday and Friday. By now he was beginning to get some real looks from the other prisoners. Everyone knew he was completely devoted to his God, but Nickolai was sure many of them had no real idea what sitting in a wooden box for 10 days at a time had to do with it. Was he a religious fanatic? a lunatic? Was he a political prisoner just trying to make a political statement?

Sooner or later Nickolai knew he was going to get an opportunity to share his story. Sooner or later someone would come asking, and Nickolai would get a chance to tell them why he was so devoted to serving his God. But for now the others just watched and wondered at Nickolai's vigilant faith.

And when the Sabbath day arrived, things turned out exactly as Nickolai knew they would. He was put back in the box.

It amazed him that the warden was sticking to this strategy of discipline. Every time he put Nickolai in the box, Nickolai was out of commission for 10 days, and then it took at least a day for him to recover and recoup his strength. That left him only two days to resume work again before being put back into the box. If the warden wanted to run an efficient camp, locking Nickolai up for such lengthy periods of time wasn't working. At least not if he wanted to get any work out of Nickolai.

The whole thing didn't make much sense, but then the whole strategy of the Soviet government didn't make much sense to Nickolai either. Why force a person or group of people to give up something they cherished? The whole thing was like trying to force a man to turn against his own family, but of course the prison warden wouldn't care about that. He had no religion. He would never comprehend the strength of Nickolai's allegiance to his God and his church family. If he had, he never would have persisted in fighting against Nickolai's incredible, immovable devotion to the service of his God.

And so it went as the short summer weeks turned into the chill of autumn. Frost came in August and then a light snow in early September. While in the box, Nickolai could not afford to sleep for very long periods of time. Every few minutes he had to wake up to move his legs and arms so he could keep the circulation going.

When the frigid days of winter came in late October, Nickolai worried. How would he stay alive? How would he manage to stay warm all cooped up in a small box?

Nickolai wasn't sure it really mattered anymore. If he perished, he perished. If it was time for him to lay down his life for Jesus, then he was at peace with such a fate.

But just as resigned as he was to this possibility, he was just as sure that God had a plan for his life—something in store for him as God's witness, though it be in a box.

It was at times like this that the Scriptures became Nickolai's greatest comfort. His favorite passages were Psalms 23, 91, and 140. These wonderful psalms helped him focus on the real battle that was raging—the battle between good and evil.

Yuri must have been feeling sorry for Nickolai again, because one morning when he brought the preacher his bread and water, he also brought two thick blankets. It had been an especially cold night, and the gesture warmed Nickolai's heart with gratefulness to Yuri and God. The blankets wouldn't keep him toasty, but they would take the edge off the cold winter nights.

All the water in camp was freezing over by now. Even the barrels of water brought from the spring on a daily basis would freeze by morning. During the early days of winter Petya, the cook, would break the thick sheet of ice at the top of each barrel in the mornings. But when the real temperatures of winter settled in and dropped to zero and below, the water froze solid in a matter of hours. Petya began having Oleg bring the barrels inside the kitchen.

Because of the extreme temperature, Nickolai knew he couldn't afford to let the water get chilled. If he allowed the water to start to freeze, it would drop his body temperature even further when he drank it. From now on he knew he would have to drink right away when Yuri brought him his can of water.

The hours of daylight were few now, and the nights longer. Nickolai's breath made puffs of steam when he breathed, and when he pulled the blanket up around his face a crust of frost quickly gathered. How he managed to stay warm in the ice-cold temperatures, he never knew, but one thing was sure—with God all things are possible. He was Nickolai's ever-present help in trouble.

Chapter 18

L ate one afternoon Yuri came into the stable quite unexpectedly. He pushed and pulled Nickolai's wooden crate to a dark corner of the stable away from the doorway and the chilly winds that sometimes blew in when the door was open.

Nickolai was surprised at the ease with which Yuri moved the box, but then he realized that he was not the stout man he once was. Even through his coat he could feel his ribs. When Yuri began forking hay up around the crate, Nickolai's heart was touched. The hay would do wonders to insulate him against the cold winter air. Now, beyond a shadow of a doubt, he knew the guard really did care what happened to him.

"Thank you" was all Nickolai said, but the two of them knew what such a gesture could truly mean to Nickolai. It would very likely save his life.

Nickolai was sure that Yuri was acting on his own and that the warden knew nothing of Yuri's thoughtful deeds. The food he had brought, the water, the blankets, and the hay piled high around his box—all were simple acts of kindness, and yet ones that couldn't be misconstrued.

The cold days of winter turned to a wet spring. Unable to move about in the box when he was imprisoned there, the damp air chilled Nickolai to the bone. He wasn't sure which was worse—the frigid, mind-numbing days of winter, or the wet bone-chilling days of spring.

When summer finally came, and his 10-day confinements in the crate continued, the insects returned and so did the memories of his first days in the box. Again his skin swelled up from the bites of mosquitoes, black flies, and no-see-ums. Surprisingly, in spite of the moderate temperatures outside, many days in the stable under the tin roof turned oppressively warm. This brought problems again with cleanliness since Nickolai was not allowed out of the box to go to the bathroom. And of course this just made the fly problem even worse.

All that summer Nickolai endured the sessions of being confined in the wooden box. All that summer he would approach the Sabbath with stubborn faithfulness and a tenacity that impressed even the warden. If Nickolai could have seen how it really affected the warden, he would have been greatly encouraged.

Nevertheless, the warden would not give in, and back Nickolai would go to the box each Sabbath. He would endure his 10-day sentence, be released, and then suffer great anguish as he worked to regain the use of his legs. Then he would spend a couple of days working with Vadeem on camp repairs and projects before being locked up again in the box.

As fall arrived and once again stretched into winter, Nickolai became known as the preacher in the box. He hated to think that his time in the box was being wasted, and some days he had to wonder what in the world God's long-range plan might be. He had heard of saints who suffered in prison for 20 and 30 years, and he dreaded the possibility of such a fate, but even that didn't seem to deter him much anymore. It seemed to be part of Nickolai's routine now, a part of who he was and who he had become.

Most days he wasn't sure which would be better—to live another day and suffer the slow painful deterioration of his body through such torture, or experience a quick death that would end his earthly life.

But again it didn't really matter. Hadn't his life already been one long trial of persecution for the sake of the gospel? Why question God's plan now? Nickolai truly did trust his heavenly Father. Someday all would be clear. In the meantime he tried not to ask too many philosophical questions about the quality of life or about God's overall plan for him. He just kept quoting scriptures that promised answers someday, and this gave him simple strength to endure for yet another day.

"All things work together for good to those who love God, to those who are the called according to His purpose" (Romans 8:28, NKJV), he would recite to himself countless times while in the box.

All the verses he had memorized in his life were coming back to him now, and they were a real source of comfort in his time of need.

"Do not fear any of those things that you are about to suffer. Indeed, the devil is about to throw some of you into prison, that you may be tested, and you will have tribulation ten days" (Revelation 2:10, NKJV). This part of the verse always made Nickolai smile ironically. He knew the verse was more symbolic than literal—but still it was satisfying to think that John the revelator had used the very number of days in the prophecy that matched the number of days Nickolai was having to suffer each time in the box.

"Be faithful until death, and I will give you the crown of life" (verse 10, NKJV). That was the part of the passage that always gave him the greatest hope. It reminded him that nothing really mattered in life except that he remain faithful to Jesus.

And so to witness for God in a Communist prison was truly a privilege. As far as Nickolai could tell, there were no Christians in the camp. He could hardly believe that, but as of yet, none had shone their true colors or dared to come forward even if just to encourage him.

But if his witness for Jesus could bring even one soul to Christ, he felt it would be worth it. All the pain and hardship he had endured would stand for something—it would not be for nothing. And who knew? If one man were brought to Jesus, maybe others would follow.

Another cold winter followed on the heels of autumn, and then spring edged its way into camp. One spring day when Nickolai was once again pulled from the box, he lay there in the straw looking out through the stable doorway. The month of May had come, and although this time of year was still quite cool, the sunshine and clear blue sky warmed his heart.

As Nickolai slowly flexed his legs, trying to get the kinks out of his knees, he thanked God for life. He thanked Jesus for the chance to be a living witness for Him instead of being a martyr. It was amazing that he could endure such hardship and not resent the leading of his heavenly Father, but it was famous lines from Scripture that always kept him upbeat in his attitude toward life. One of his favorites was from the writings of Paul.

"For I have learned in whatever state I am, to be content" (Philippians 4:11, NKJV).

And that of course was what always made the difference. How could it not? Nickolai had given his life totally to God, and God was giving him just what he needed day by day until the time was right to reveal the next phase of His divine plan.

Chapter 19

A few weeks later unusual guests showed up at the prison camp. Three military officers rode in on horses, and it was obvious by their appearance that one of them was a high-ranking colonel in the army—all the way from Nizhny Novgorod.

It soon became clear that they were there to inspect the camp. The warden pulled out all the stops and made quite a show of things—not that he had anything remarkable to brag about at the prison camp. It was a standard camp out in the middle of nowhere on the Siberian steppes, housing some 300 prisoners, with no notorious or political criminals among them.

But guests at the camp were rare, so giving these special visitors a tour was the biggest thing that had happened at the camp in years. They were shown the officers' quarters, the kitchen and mess hall, and the barracks. Nickolai could hear their conversation as the tour took them near the stables.

"What's in here?" the colonel asked, pointing at the low-roofed shed where Nickolai's box was kept.

The warden glanced through the open doorway of the stable. He had put Nickolai in the box just three days ago, but he had hoped to avoid having to explain the situation to the colonel.

"Oh, this is where we house the worst prisoners," he said nonchalantly. "Severe punishment keeps the insubordinate ones under control."

"What types of punishment?"

"Oh, various types." The warden squirmed.

The officer stepped through the doorway and peered into the dim shadows of the stable.

"We keep them locked up in boxes like that one." The warden pointed at Nickolai's wooden crate in the corner.

"How many prisoners are locked up right now?" The officer was painfully persistent, and Nickolai could sense the uneasiness in the warden's voice.

"Well, we have only one man in here right now."

"And he's in for what, specifically?"

"For refusing to carry out his duties."

The officer stepped closer to the wooden crate, but immediately stepped back as his nose caught a whiff of the foul stench coming from the crate.

"Whew!" he exclaimed. "And how long have you been punishing him for this sort of insubordination?"

"H'mmm," the warden scratched his head. "Only three days this time, so far, but he's in for a 10-day stint."

"A 10-day stint?" the colonel looked skeptical. "And you say he won't work? How many times has he been insubordinate?"

"Well—now—he's been giving us trouble ever since he arrived in camp." The warden's eyes darted back and forth between the box and the colonel. "Every time we let him out, he disobeys again, so we just put him back in the box."

The colonel looked at the box again. "And you've tried this how many times?"

"H'mmm—I guess—uh, we've been doing it for pretty close to two years now."

The colonel looked at the warden incredulously, his mouth dropping open in disbelief.

Through the cracks in the crate Nickolai watched the whole thing transpire, and with bated breath he waited for the conversation to continue. It was becoming more and more apparent that the colonel did not approve of such crude forms of treatment, and it also appeared as though the warden was about to get reprimanded for it.

"Two years?"

"Yes, sir."

"You've had this man locked up in this tiny box for 10-day stints repeatedly during the past two years? That must be some 40 or 50 times at least!"

The warden looked embarrassed. He paused, and then finally replied, "Well, yes, I'd say that's about right."

"Do you mean to tell me that you've been locking this man up in this crate for two years, and it hasn't done any good? that even with this type of punishment, he's still being disobedient, or insubordinate, or whatever you want to call it?" The colonel was getting more irritated by the minute. "Did it ever occur to you, officer, that there may be a good reason this man isn't following your orders? I mean, two years, and he still hasn't come around!"

The warden looked shocked and bewildered and aghast all in the same instant.

"Well, did you?"

"No—no, sir! It didn't occur to me just like that—but now that you put it that way, it does sound pretty ridiculous!"

"Ridiculous!" the colonel almost shouted. "I'll say it sounds ridiculous! Totally idiotic, if you ask me! In fact, I'm beginning to question who the intelligent one is around here! Certainly not you!" He continued to glare at the warden. "I ought to have your commission revoked for running such an operation! This isn't discipline! It's just plain torture! We Russian officers may be tough and mean as wildcats, but we're not animals!"

Chapter 20

The colonel abruptly turned back to the crate. "Open the box!" he ordered, his voice still livid with anger. "Open the box at once!"

Yuri came forward and opened the lock that held the latch. He lifted the lid and reached into the box to help Nickolai stand to his feet.

It had been only three days since Nickolai had been put into the box, but by now his legs were already like rubber. He tried to stand without wavering, but he couldn't. The strength was just not there. With so few days between the stints in the box, he had slowly lost the ability to recuperate quickly, and each time his legs would atrophy a little more.

"Here! Lay him in this pile of straw over here!" the colonel barked. "And get him a drink of water!" He waved his hand to ward off the flies and the stench that was permeating the shed.

"And bring a bucket of water so he can clean himself up!" The colonel turned to Nickolai and shook his head again. "What's your name, young man?"

"Panchuk, sir. Nickolai Panchuk."

The officer continued looking kindly at Nickolai. "Is it true that you won't work?"

"No. It's not true." Nickolai swallowed some of the water from the cup Yuri handed him. "I will work. I'll work harder than all the other prisoners, if need be. I'll get up early and stay up late every night, but—but I can't dishonor God and work on His holy Sabbath day."

The colonel raised his eyebrows.

"The seventh day of every week is God's *Subota*," Nickolai continued, seeing the opportunity to witness once again about his beloved Sabbath. "I was raised to keep it holy, and I can't violate my conscience, sir! On the seventh day of each week I can't work, because it would be disobeying the commands of my God."

Nickolai wanted to be respectful of the officer, but right now he was lying in a pile of straw. It was hard to stand at attention or salute the colonel while lying prostrate on the stable floor. The nervousness showed on his face.

"At ease, prisoner," came the colonel's reassuring command as he stared down at Nickolai. "What did you do for a living before you came to this camp?"

"I was a pastor, sir. It's why I was sent here in the first place—because I wouldn't turn over a list of my church members to the KGB." Nickolai's voice wavered and then almost broke with emotion as he added, "I could not, sir! It would have betrayed the confidence my members had placed in me as their spiritual leader."

Nickolai felt strange. Why was he baring his soul to this unknown army officer? He felt chagrined and relieved at the same time. He couldn't explain it, but somehow it seemed the right thing to do at this point.

"So you will work, but you won't work on Saturdays? Your *Subota,* as you call it?"

"Yes, sir. I'll work hard, before sunup and well after dark, to make up for the time I miss on Saturdays."

The colonel looked at the warden. "Do you have a job like this? One that can be done on some days and not others? A job that can be done in fewer days if this man works more hours each of the other days?"

The warden thought for a long moment. "Well, there is the water that needs to be brought from the spring a kilometer away." He glanced at the colonel. "We need barrels of water, and it usually takes a man and ox seven days of hauling to bring enough water for the camp. Enough for drinking water, cooking, and any washing the men need to do."

The warden looked at Nickolai lying in the straw and then at the colonel. "I suppose we could give that a try. The man doing it now works from dawn to dusk and barely has time enough to bring the nine or 10 barrels of water we need on average per day. If Panchuk wants to get up and work before dawn each day and then work after dark, maybe he can manage to bring enough by Friday night. I doubt it, but we can give it a try." The warden had a cynical look in his eye, but he chose his words carefully in front of the colonel.

The officer brightened. "All right, then, Panchuk. It's a deal. Let's see what you can do. Tomorrow is Tuesday. The warden says that if you can bring enough water by Friday night, you can have your day off. Five days of work in four. If you can do it, then Saturday is a free day."

And then the colonel got a serious look in his eye as he looked straight at Nickolai. "But if you can't keep up your end of the bargain, you're going to have to haul water on Saturdays, too. Your *Subota*, as you call it. Are we clear on this?"

"Absolutely."

"I'm curious, Panchuk." The colonel searched Nickolai's face—although it was filled with pain, it held the peace of heaven.

"You have been so stubborn in refusing to work on your *Subota*," he continued. "What happens if Saturday comes and you still don't have enough water? We've got a deal, and yet somehow I get the feeling that you would probably still choose to go into the box than work and violate your holy day."

Nickolai thought about the question before answering the kindest Russian military officer he had ever met. He chose his words carefully because he wanted to honor the colonel's faith in him and the warden's willingness to give him a chance to prove himself.

"If I honor my God, He will honor me, sir. He knows I wish to worship Him in prayer and quiet meditation on that day, so I am placing my confidence in Him, that He will give me the strength to complete the challenge. I will work half the night, if need be, just to complete my part of the bargain and secure for myself the right to worship my God on that day."

"You know, I believe you will," the colonel nodded and smiled kindly. The man's generosity made Nickolai feel warm inside, and it gave him hope that everything would turn out for the best after all. It seemed that this was the break he had been hoping for, the chance he had been wanting for two years—a chance to show everyone the sovereignty of his God.

Nickolai rested the remainder of the day, trying to limber up and get his knees to work again. By nightfall he felt pretty good; however, as he lay on his bunk that night in the barracks, he thought about the distance to the spring. It had to be more than a half mile (one kilometer). That would be almost a mile and a half (two and a half kilometers) each round trip. Nickolai figured it would take maybe two and a half to three hours for each load of water.

From what he had seen, the oxcart carried two barrels at a time, so that meant he needed to haul five loads a day to bring the quota of water per day. But he needed to haul enough water for Saturday's supply too. There was no question about it—Nickolai knew he was going to have to haul at least one or two extra loads a day to make it!

With his mind whirling, he took time to pray before dozing off. *Lord, help me not to worry. Help me to have the energy I need to take on this amazing challenge. It is truly a challenge straight from the courts of heaven!*

Chapter 21

Before dawn had even lit the eastern sky the next morning, Nickolai was out at the stables helping Oleg, the oxcart driver, hitch up old Maksim. Oleg would be working with Nickolai for the day, to teach him the routine of hauling water from the spring.

Nickolai knew that this was his chance to win Sabbath privileges and be a powerful witness for God. For two years he had been confined repeatedly in a wooden box for 10 days at a time because he wouldn't work on the Sabbath. But he had remained true to his convictions and suffered everything the warden could throw at him.

Now God had provided Nickolai a way of escape from the torture box with his faith still intact. It was time for Nickolai to witness in a different sort of way.

There was so much at stake. Would God help Nickolai do what seemed to be an impossibility? Could Nickolai and Maksim haul seven days' worth of water in just six days of work each week? And this week the task was even more daunting—five days' worth of water in four.

In Nickolai's mind it would take a miracle, but that was, of course, what God was all about. It was what Nickolai's busy life as a pastor had been all about. It was what his interrogation episodes with the KGB had been about, his eventual sentence at this prison camp, and his confinement in the box for refusing to work on the Sabbath day. And it was what his release and new assignment with Maksim were all about. Nickolai's life of sacrifice and service to God had been one miracle after another, and Nickolai doubted that the miracles would stop now. There was too much at stake.

And so it was that Nickolai and Oleg set out for the spring across the treeless steppes. It took them more than an hour to make the trek as they walked along laboriously behind the plodding ox.

"Can't we make this old ox hurry any faster!" Nickolai complained as the oxcart lumbered slowly along past muskegs and around bogs. "If he walks this slow all day, we'll never get our five loads in by the end of today!"

"Oh, we'll get the water in, all right, but old Maksim has never promised me that we'd do it before dark. Often we come trudging in long after dark. You should know that! You were there in the shed to witness it lots of times!"

Nickolai stared at Oleg, a stunned look settling in on his face. If they couldn't manage the regular number of loads in a given day, how were they going to be able to get the extra barrels of water hauled to camp?

Oleg just shook his head. "I guess you thought this was going to be an easy job!" he snorted.

"Uh, no, not actually, but I was hoping we would be able to get Maksim to move along a little faster."

Oleg made a face, and shook his head again. "Look! I'm sorry that you had to stay cooped up in that box, and I'm glad the colonel let you out, but this business of getting more barrels of water so you can have your day off is crazy. Old Maksim here knows nothing about any of that. All he knows is that when he wants to walk, he walks. And when he wants to walk slower, there's nothing you can do to hurry him up!"

Nickolai wanted to say something, but he didn't.

"I know what you're thinking!" Oleg kept on. "You were thinking that since you're a preacher man, your God would work some kind of miracle! I'm right, aren't I?" Oleg gave the ox a slap on his rump.

"You thought your God would reach down out of the sky above and tickle old Maksim's ear or something to make him move faster, didn't you! And then Maksim would run like nobody's business and have all the water for the week hauled to the camp in six days! Hey! Maybe even in five?"

Oleg was still shaking his head. His reaction seemed logical enough. Should Nickolai have expected anything less? He had thought that the other prisoners might admire him for standing up for what he believed in, but maybe that wasn't the case at all. Maybe they had no respect for a man who wouldn't work, especially if he was asking for one day of work off in seven? All the men were working hard, and they were all being held at this prison camp against their will. Then too, like the warden, they didn't know a thing about Nickolai's God or the devotion he had for his Maker.

Nickolai had nothing more to say, so he walked the remainder of the distance in silence. What was the use?

The first rays of sunshine were just beginning to peek over the horizon when they arrived at the spring. Nickolai helped Oleg dip wooden buckets into the pool of water at the spring and then pour them into the barrels waiting on the oxcart.

It wasn't a hard task, but several times Nickolai sloshed water from the buckets on himself. The morning air was still chilly, and the cold water made Nickolai shiver. He realized that if he wanted to stay dry he was going to have to learn how to put more water into the barrels and less on himself. Besides, if he were careless, it would take that much longer to fill the barrels.

Oleg put the wooden lids on the two barrels and then nudged Maksim forward with his ox goad. Nickolai was glad to see that Oleg no longer used his leather prod to beat Maksim. He used the goad instead to guide the ox and send him signals as to what he wanted him to do.

The trip back to camp took even longer since the cart was loaded down with full barrels of water. Several times Nickolai tried to urge Maksim along faster, but always the old ox resisted his efforts. In fact, any attempts to hurry him along seemed to make him move slower.

If Nickolai could have gotten into the harness to help Maksim pull the cart along faster, he thought he would gladly do it. As it was, he and Oleg were at the mercy of Maksim and his whims to move along at his own pace. In the end Nickolai realized Oleg was right—there was nothing they could do but walk along patiently beside the cart.

Chapter 22

At the camp they worked to unload the barrels from the cart, trying to avoid spilling any of the precious water. It was a simple routine, but Nickolai wanted to get on the road again. Unfortunately, as they began the process all over again neither Maksim nor Oleg seemed in any hurry to move at a pace that suited Nickolai.

By now Nickolai was beginning to feel that he would rather work by himself than have Oleg along. In fact, he was sure of it. As the two of them filled the barrels for the second time and then turned old Maksim around for the trip back to camp, Nickolai began to form a plan.

Why tie up the time of two men doing a job that could be done by one? The job was turning out to be much easier than Nickolai had anticipated. Old Maksim was doing most of the work anyway.

Nickolai waited to speak his mind until after they had unloaded the two barrels of water at the kitchen.

"I've been thinking," Nickolai ventured. "It's a long way out to the spring, and it seems a terrible waste of manpower to have us both walking all the way out there. You've taught me what I need to know, and now the rest is up to Maksim. Why don't you let me try a run by myself? If I have any trouble, I can let you know when I get back."

Nickolai wiped the sweat from his forehead with his sleeve and ran his hand through his hair. "Do you think that would work?"

"H'mmm—you're probably right," Oleg admitted as he stared at the empty water barrels they had just loaded onto the cart. He stole a glance at Nickolai. "You'll probably have no trouble."

And so Nickolai began his new job solo, and he put his energy into it. As soon as he was out of earshot, he began to do his best to get Maksim to increase his speed. But old Maksim didn't appreciate being hurried along. A few times Nickolai tried whipping him up a bit with the goad, but after a few hundred yards (few hundred meters) of this, old Maksim slowed his pace down to almost a standstill.

In the end Nickolai realized once again the truth of what Oleg had said—old Maksim just couldn't be made to run faster. He would walk when he wanted to, and he would stop when he wanted to. And short of beating the ox mercilessly, it wasn't going to change things any.

They made several more trips out to the spring, but as the day wound down, so did Maksim's energy. Near the end he was walking slower and slower. Now Nickolai was really frustrated, and if the whole thing hadn't been so pathetic, he might have laughed.

To Nickolai it was obvious that Maksim didn't care how many loads he could get in before dark. He was just an animal. But animal or not, in some ways it appeared that Maksim was just another one of the prisoners. He was being forced to work against his will—harnessed to a cart every morning and made to walk back and forth all day to the spring. That was the life of a prisoner in a prison camp, wasn't it? Work, work, work.

Like machines, Nickolai and Maksim would spend each day working as though that was what they had been made to do. They might not like it, but they would do it anyway, because that was what everyone did out here on the windswept steppes of Siberia.

But all of that was just rhetoric. At the end of each day Nickolai needed to have more than his quota of five cartloads of water in camp—by the end of the week he needed 10 extra barrels of water or he was going to have to go through more pain and alienation in the box. This was his one chance! This was the opportunity Nickolai had been longing for during the two years he had been cooped up in the wooden crate.

So whether Maksim felt like moving fast or not, they needed to get that extra water in by Friday evening. If they had to haul water half the night, they were going to do it. Nickolai was going to prove to the warden that working hard and having a Sabbath day's rest was possible. He wanted Yuri to know it, and Oleg, and any other person in camp who witnessed his persistent loyalty to the Sabbath and his God.

But by the time the shadows were long on the Siberian landscape, Nickolai knew it wasn't enough. He was going to have to work after dark. The sun was low in the sky as the fifth cartload rumbled into camp, and he knew he needed at least one more load tonight if he was going to make a dent in the 10 extra barrels he needed by Friday night.

When Nickolai had finished unloading the barrels, he turned the cart around quickly and headed out of camp for one more trip to the spring. But Maksim had other ideas. He pulled the cart off the road and toward the stables just 40 or 50 yards (40 or 50 meters) away. Not to be outdone, Nickolai pulled hard to the left to steer Maksim back onto the road.

It was a battle of man against beast, brain against brute. Maksim wasn't used to going back out to the spring this time of night, but Nickolai knew they had to have that extra load of water. Nickolai used the goad to persuade Maksim.

"Can't you get it into your thick skull that I'm doing this for your own good!" Nickolai half shouted. "I'm just as tired as you are," he added with a stubborn resolution that surprised even himself, "but it doesn't matter! We're going to do this whether we like it or not!"

Nickolai felt bad yelling at Maksim like that. The old ox was tired. He had worked all day pulling that cart back and forth from the spring. They had already hauled five loads of water and walked what Nickolai figured was more than seven miles (12 kilometers). And now they were going to walk another mile and a half (two to three kilometers), and put in another two to three hours of work.

He wished that he could somehow convey the idea to Maksim that a day of rest for the man on Sabbath would be a day of rest for the ox. But he guessed that he would have to leave that job up to God. Only the Creator truly knew how to do that.

Chapter 23

The next morning Nickolai was up before everyone. He was up before any of the prisoners had stirred, and before the warden or guards. He was up before even the cook had begun to stoke the fires in the kitchen. But the sun was already peeking over the horizon, and Nickolai guessed it must be about 4:00 a.m.

He was a little weary from the short night, and his legs were a bit stiff, but he flexed them again and again to limber them up. He couldn't afford to sleep in or slack off now. He needed to be up and going, out on that road to the spring so he could get enough water barrels hauled in by Friday.

The sun wasn't up yet. It hadn't even begun to rise in the east as Nickolai threw on his clothes, grabbed a flask of water, and went to the stables to rouse old Maksim. Of course the hour was earlier than Maksim was accustomed to, but Nickolai managed to get him on his feet and into his harness.

The old ox eyed Nickolai warily, as if he were suspicious of the man's every move. And why shouldn't he be? This man was crazy! Urging him to hurry all day long, pushing him to work all hours of the night, and now he was getting the ox up and out of the stable at an unearthly hour.

Nickolai was in a hurry to get going. He didn't think he had time to eat a regular breakfast, but he did stop by the kitchen for a carryout meal. The cook was up by now and gave him some bread and carrots to take with him. Nickolai knew he could stop by the kitchen later that morning for some hot borsch and Russian bread, but for now the cold food would have to do.

The man and ox headed west out of the camp and toward the spring. Maksim knew the way even in the dark. He could walk the distance himself without anyone guiding him—he would have even been able to make the trip with Nickolai sleeping in the back of the oxcart. Unfortunately, there wasn't room in the cart. The barrels were too big and took up all the space.

The morning was peaceful at this hour, with the silence of nature all around them. The only sound that broke the stillness of the morning was the creaking of old Maksim's harness and the squeaking wheels on the oxcart. Other than that there was little to punctuate the early-morning hour.

In the pale light of predawn Nickolai could see a few lemmings come out of the burrows they had made for themselves in the matted sedge grass lining the roadway. A little farther along he saw a snowy owl perched on a craggy rock poking its way through the Siberian landscape. And of course there were the snowshoe hares, now brown with their summer camouflage.

At one point Nickolai rounded a bend in the road and suddenly caught his breath. Sitting in the middle of the road was a large wolf, his lanky body tall and lean—Nickolai guessed he was about three feet tall at the shoulder. And he just sat there staring at the man and ox.

Maksim pulled to a stop for a few tense moments. It was obvious the ox didn't really know what to do. Nickolai sensed he was frightened, because he could see the muscles ripple and tighten in the ox's neck and shoulders.

Did Nickolai need to worry? Was this wolf out scouting for a meal? Would he come back with others from his wolf pack? The wolf finally got up and trotted off to the north. Nickolai breathed a little easier after the wolf left. No one had alerted him to the possibility of wolf attacks out here, and he and Oleg hadn't encountered the wolf the previous day.

He consoled himself with the idea that the wolf was probably not a threat to them anyway. There were plenty of lemmings and snowshoe hares for the wolf to hunt and eat. Of course, when the harsh winter struck Siberia come October, Nickolai was not sure where he and the ox would rank on the food chain for a hungry pack of wolves.

Food was not exactly abundant in this deserted country. The only other sizable game on the steppes of Siberia would be reindeer that traveled in scattered herds. Or so he had been told when he asked Petya, the cook, during a conversation with him in the kitchen one evening.

Chapter 24

It had been on one of those days months back when Nickolai had just gotten out of the box and was trying to recuperate. He had managed to hobble to the kitchen late in the day to get something to eat. After the evening meal he had stayed late and helped Petya scrub the pots and pans and prepare some sourdough for baking the next morning.

They worked in silence until Petya began talking about cooking and the limited supply of ingredients he had in the camp. He was hoping for some reindeer meat that winter.

"The reindeer herds come this way some years—other years we never see them," Petya had said as he covered the sourdough with a towel and set it aside. "When they do come, and we can shoot a few, we lay aside enough meat for a good long while. Fifteen or 20 reindeer is a lot of meat, but of course it doesn't go far with 300 men in camp."

Petya glanced at Nickolai and raised his eyebrows. "I suppose you're wondering where the guns are that they use to hunt the reindeer."

"Well, I hadn't thought of that, but now that you mention it, I haven't seen any guns in camp."

"That's because they don't bring the guns out unless the reindeer herds come this way. I think they must keep the rifles locked up in the warden's office or something. No one really knows. I've never been told." He continued, "Of course they give the rifles only to the guards, but no one really gives it much thought. Everyone is just glad to get some meat to eat—reindeer meat is pretty good eating."

Petya began to hang the pots and pans up to dry, and Nickolai did what he could to help. "If the reindeer don't come this way, then we have to satisfy ourselves with the cabbage, turnips, beets, and onions we grow in our gardens. They keep pretty well, and in cold weather we can store them underground in beds of hay."

Nickolai thought about the vegetables that Petya cooked up in the borsch—cabbage and beets mostly. Borsch was something every Russian ate every day. Not to have borsch for a main meal was considered almost unthinkable.

Petya had big forearms from his work in the kitchen. Making bread, cutting up turnips and beets, and scrubbing pots and pans could do that to you. He was a quiet man and didn't appear to have many friends. But he was a great cook—everybody said so.

"You're a good cook, Petya," Nicholai found himself saying, "especially with the limited resources you have to work with."

"You just say that because you don't know any better," Petya insisted, laughing good-naturedly, and Nickolai found himself laughing too. "You've been locked up in the box too long. You're always hungry, and anything that hits your tongue tastes good to you," Petya added.

Nickolai's reminiscing ended when he reached the spring. As he filled the water barrels, the sun finally rose in all its glory. He worked quickly to finish the job, and then turned Maksim and the oxcart around. It felt like they were making progress, and Maksim was responding well to the urgency Nickolai felt.

At this pace Nickolai was sure they would be able to bring home six loads of water—12 barrels. And who knew? Maybe they would be able to do even more than that. In Nickolai's mind seven trips to the spring was not out of the question.

All that morning Nickolai drove the ox hard, never letting up with the stick, never allowing the ox to rest or pause by the road for a little sedge grass. Today was Wednesday. If he could manage to get 14 barrels of water into the camp by bedtime, and another 14 on Thursday, he would have to get only 10 on Friday. That would give him time to get home and prepare properly for the Sabbath when it was time for the sun to set.

But Nickolai was getting way ahead of himself, and he had misjudged the nature of a beast of burden. As morning turned to afternoon and the sun turned west, old Maksim began to slow his pace. His shoulders sagged a little more, and his tongue began to hang out when they stopped at the spring or at the camp to unload the full barrels. Of course Nickolai let the ox have a good long drink while he was filling the barrels at the spring. That was efficiency at its best. Why not give Maksim a chance to rest, and drink his fill while Nickolai was busy filling the water barrels?

But when they were back in camp, Nickolai paused only long enough for Petya to hand him some bread and a tin bowlful of red borsch. At these times Nickolai never gave Maksim a chance to get more than a short drink.

And so they plodded on, with Maksim growing more tired each hour and slower with each leg of each trip. By late afternoon it was obvious that pushing Maksim hard had sapped the ox's stamina and his willingness to keep going. In fact, the fifth trip to the spring took more than three hours. The sun was so low in the sky now that Nickolai could see they were going to be hard pressed to get six loads of water— they would have to work long after dark again to do it.

He was so frustrated with Maksim as the time slipped away, but what could he do? He determined that he would simply have to drive the ox harder! He had no other choice! They would have to go faster to get the water in by Sabbath! Nickolai had come too far in his plan to let it go now!

With a stronger resolve, Nickolai vowed to make Maksim work if it was the last thing he did on earth! But Nickolai knew that if this was going to really happen, something was going to have to change! He was going to have to reshape the way Maksim did things. To modify an animal's behavior, you had to force him to obey, either by punishing him for wrong behavior or by rewarding him for obedience.

He cringed as he suddenly realized that this was exactly what the warden had been trying to do with him. The warden had been stubbornly putting him in the wooden crate, trying to break him.

"Is that what I'm doing to you?" Nickolai asked incredulously as he stared at Maksim. "Is that what this is all about?"

The lemmings along the roadside stopped their squeaking and sat up to hear more of the debate. The snowshoe hares browsing on the short sedge grasses perked up their ears to hear the final verdict.

For a long moment Nickolai gave the idea some thought, but then just as suddenly he snapped out of his reverie.

"There's no time for that now!" he argued, his mind seesawing back in the other direction. "I don't have time to be feeling sorry for an ox that doesn't want to work hard. If I can do it, then he can do it too!"

Nickolai didn't let up. "I'll push you all day, Maksim, and all night if I need to! I'll go without meals—I'll go without sleep!"

In frustration he whacked Maksim on the rump with the goad, and the old ox jumped forward. Maksim was going to work hard all day every day—Nickolai would see to that!

Of course, at the end of the week Maksim was going to get the Sabbath off just as Nickolai was. The pastor smiled in spite of his irritation. Any rest for Nickolai would be a rest for Maksim. The old ox didn't know it yet, but he would soon enough. Come Sabbath he would be lying in the stable enjoying the sedge grass piled high in his feeding trough.

Chapter 25

On Thursday morning Nickolai was up even earlier than the day before. But his worst fears from the day before had been realized—try as he might, he had managed to haul only six loads of water.

As he thought about how hard he had worked until long after dark, the whole thing was disheartening. What else did he need to do that he had not already done? Short of giving up, there seemed no answers.

When Nickolai went to the stables, Maksim seemed listless and tired, as though he had already used up the day's ration of energy. As they headed out of camp, the old ox walked with his head down and no light in his eyes. He didn't even look Nickolai's way when the man tried to give him his favorite snack—a carrot.

Nickolai knew he was now paying the price for pushing Maksim to the limit two days in a row. And in some sad sort of way it seemed only right. He had ignored the common-sense logic and the goodness in his heart that said he should be kinder to the animal. Justice in nature's law of averages had prevailed, and Nickolai couldn't deny that it should be so.

Hour after hour the ox plodded slowly along with no sense of the urgency Nickolai felt. He had worked overtime two days in a row, and now it seemed that he was thinking he deserved to slow things down a bit. After all, it wasn't his neck on the line. Why should he work faster simply to trade one day for another? Of course he had no knowledge of Nickolai's Sabbath or the importance of the standoff between the preacher and the warden.

The sun passed its zenith as morning turned to afternoon. White cumulus clouds scudded across the landscape now green with the short grasses of summer growth. A few white cardamine flowers stared up at the man and ox as they passed by with the creaking water cart.

Suddenly the lone wolf came out to watch them again. This time he sat on a slight rise to the south, following their every move as though the man and beast were the best source of entertainment he had seen in days.

But Nickolai hardly noticed them. He was growing more and more discouraged by the hour. All his efforts to work hard and deliver the quota of barrels by sunset Friday were going to be to no avail. It just wasn't going to be enough. Nickolai could feel it in his bones. There wasn't enough time.

Nickolai filled the barrels for the third time that day, and then turned the cart around again. As he trudged along the road, Nickolai did the math one more time. Ten barrels of water per day were needed—50 by Friday night so that he wouldn't have to haul any on the Sabbath. Two barrels of water per trip meant that he needed to make 25 trips in just four days.

With the six loads he hauled on Tuesday and the six on Wednesday, he would need a total of 13 more. That meant he would need seven at least for today, and then maybe six for Friday.

How was he going to be able to do it? He hadn't managed to bring in seven loads either of the other two days, and today Maksim was working even slower. Seven loads seemed impossible.

To be sure, at this rate they'd never make it by sundown Friday. If he had begun working on Sunday, maybe he would have been able to make one extra trip per day. Maybe then he could have gotten the number of barrels needed by Friday night.

By now old Maksim was even limping a bit, and his pace had slowed to little more than a crawl. Nickolai finally stopped the old ox and examined his foot. The foot had picked up a rock, so Nickolai removed it.

He stood up and sighed before slapping Maksim on the hindquarters. There was no longer any point in using the ox goad to urge Maksim along. He simply let the ox go at his own pace.

Evening finally came, putting both Nickolai and Maksim out of their misery. They had managed only five loads from the spring. Ten barrels of water—that was a good day's work, but not nearly enough to move them closer to Nickolai's goal.

Nickolai's confidence was waning. He had thought a Sabbath day's rest would be a sure thing. Didn't God want him to have His Sabbath off? So what had gone wrong? Why hadn't things worked out between him and old Maksim? Why hadn't God helped him get the number of loads he needed to fill his quota by Friday night? Did God have other plans? Did God want him to spend another 10 days in the box? Had that been His original plan for Nickolai all along?

Nickolai's brow knit in a furrowed frown. It didn't matter. He knew he wouldn't work on Sabbath even with the ultimatum from the warden hanging over his head.

There just seemed no way out! No way to turn!

Chapter 26

By now Nickolai had no idea what God had in store. He was at a total loss as to what he should expect, or what he should do next.

Sixteen barrels of water. There was no way he could haul that many by sunset the next day—10 for Friday, and then the extra six to make up the 10 he would need for the Sabbath supply. There just wasn't time.

Nickolai had been doing his part all week, but it didn't seem to him that God was doing His. He had not answered Nickolai's prayers—at least not yet, and certainly not in the way Nickolai would have thought things should go. And from all appearances it looked as though the window of opportunity was closing fast.

The whole thing left Nickolai totally discouraged. Would he get to have his Sabbaths off? His faith wanted to say yes, but his logic said no. He had worked late Wednesday, and then well after dark again on Thursday, but with only four extra barrels of water to show for it.

Nickolai spent a long time on his knees in earnest prayer that night, even losing precious sleep to talk to his heavenly Father. He had to find a way to solve his dilemma. He had to succeed somehow.

Eventually he dropped off into a troubled sleep. Somewhere in the night he awoke, still on his knees in prayer.

As Nickolai climbed onto his bunk, a sudden thought struck him full in the face. Could it be that all his efforts to bring the water to the camp had been done on his own terms? Was it possible that he had been so anxious to earn a Sabbath day's rest that he had begun to rely on his own efforts to get it?

A Bible story came to mind, and Nickolai wondered if his situation might be proving to be somewhat similar.

God had called Gideon to lead the Israelite tribes against a common enemy, the Amalekites. The Israelites had rallied to arms, answering Gideon's call by the thousands. In fact, 32,000 of them had come, anxious for battle and ready to serve. Or were they?

Evidently God saw things differently than Gideon did.

Two different tests were given—first, Gideon was told to send soldiers home if they were the least bit afraid, and second, all but 300 men were asked to leave because they weren't really ready for battle.

Gideon was dismayed that God expected so much with so little to work with, and that's exactly how Nickolai was feeling right now. How was he going to keep the Sabbath day holy if he didn't even have time, or the ox, on his side?

Nickolai half-smiled a crooked grin in the darkness. Right now he would be glad if he could have had 300 oxen on his side.

He turned over and tried to go to sleep. Like Gideon, Nickolai was beginning to realize that even if it were possible to bring in enough loads by Friday sunset, the triumph and the credit were not to be his. He had wanted to do things his way, not that his motive and intentions hadn't been pure. It was just that the plans had all been his.

He knew that God wanted him to have Sabbath off. There was no question about that. From the day Nickolai had arrived at the prison camp, he had been honoring the Sabbath. And he had suffered for it, but Nickolai thanked God every day that he had never given in and given up his loyalty to God's holy day.

But the testing time was evidently not over. This time around he wasn't being tested by being cooped up in a prison box. It was a different sort of test—one that required incredible amounts of energy and determination and patience.

But in the end he knew the victory would be God's. God was no doubt working things out for an even greater purpose than Nickolai could imagine. It had to be that! What else could it be?

If Nickolai was being tested like Gideon, then it must be that his own plans would have to give way to God's plans. The way Nickolai had been doing things left little chance for the men in camp to give God credit for anything resembling a miracle. But Nickolai was now beginning to see that if God had things His way, they wouldn't have a choice.

It felt good to surrender everything to God once again. Nickolai had always believed in giving God full control. It was like second nature to him, and he lamented the fact that he had allowed himself to get off track.

Somewhere just before Nickolai dropped off to sleep, his mind drifted once again to one of his favorite Bible verses: "All things work together for good to those who love God, who are the called according to His purpose" (Romans 8:28, NKJV).

Chapter 27

Morning came too early for Nickolai. After all the moments of discouragement during the previous two days of work, Nickolai had begun to falter in his faith.

And then he remembered that he had awakened in the night to a moment of inspiration, an amazing epiphany that his experience was actually very biblical. Like Gideon, Nickolai once again realized that he was going to have to trust in his heavenly Father. He was going to have to place his faith in the one who could make all things work together for good.

The day and the ultimate challenge had arrived, and Nickolai went out to meet them. He hurried to the barn to rouse old Maksim to the task of the day. But to his surprise, Maksim was already on his feet, his legs restless and his eyes fully alert.

"Well, well, this is a change!" Nickolai mused. "You're never on your feet this early in the morning!" He gave the old ox a swat on the rump. Every day this week when he had come to the stables, he always found Maksim lying down.

But now Maksim was yanking at his chain, ready to go.

Nickolai threw old Maksim's harness over his neck and back and strapped it on. "All right, old boy!" he announced cheerfully. "Let's get going!"

For a moment Nickolai's heart lifted at the thought of Maksim's high energy level. It was encouraging and even refreshing to see the animal finally in sync with the man. Of course, it was a bit late now, Nickolai mused to himself.

But when Nickolai led Maksim out of the shed and

hitched him to the cart, the animal lurched forward as though he were on his way to a race. Nickolai would have liked to stop by the kitchen for some cold turnips and Russian bread as he had other mornings this week, but he never had a chance. Old Maksim headed out of camp at a run, and it was all Nickolai could do to keep up with him. In fact, Nickolai ended up running all the way to the spring behind Maksim and the bouncing, bumping cart.

When Maksim finally pulled the cart to a stop, his tongue was hanging out, and his soft beige coat was wet with sweat. Nickolai tried to catch his breath as he stepped up to the ox, now also breathing heavily.

"Wow! What was that all about!" was all Nickolai could say as Maksim stood with his head down, his eyes rolling up in his head.

Nickolai filled the water barrels and then pulled a rope from the cart and tied the barrels on securely. In case Maksim got any ideas about running again, Nickolai wanted the barrels to stay on the cart.

He looked at the ox again. What was up with the big animal? The day before the whole operation had nearly come to a grinding halt because Maksim had no energy. Now he had enough energy for 10 oxen, and it appeared that he was running to beat all records. It was as though someone had built a fire under him.

Nickolai knew he couldn't afford to stand around wondering about this amazing spectacle that had occurred before his very eyes. He needed to capitalize on the opportunity Maksim was offering—the gift that God had given him.

Nickolai quickly put the wooden lids on the barrels. The old ox had made the trip in such a short time that Nickolai had to wonder just how fast it had been.

But he didn't have any time to think about it, because suddenly, as if on cue, the ox started out again. He strained against the harness until the cart was rumbling along at a fairly good pace. The old ox was moving at unheard-of speeds.

But the most bizarre thing about it all was the way Maksim was doing it. His big angular body was gliding along as if in fluid motion. His gait, steady and smooth, pulled the cart along without the lurching motion that usually came because of the play between the harness and the cart shafts.

And then suddenly Nickolai remembered a dream that he had had at the beginning of the week about Maksim and him racing to the spring. It had all been a wonderful fantasy then. Now it was an exciting reality.

Nickolai knew he had never seen anything quite like this. It was remarkable how the old animal had run to the spring on the first trip, but the return trip was even more incredible! No one would believe him if he told them. They would have had to see it even to comprehend it. How could he explain to them the peculiar sight of the ox trotting briskly along with heavy water barrels on a cart on an empty road in the wastelands of Siberia? The whole thing was just uncanny!

And now he and Maksim were making incredible time! The old ox ran and ran and ran! There was no doubt in Nickolai's mind that God was the source of Maksim's boundless energy. It was wonderful to see God demonstrating Himself in this miraculous way. It was truly a marvel and an inspiration to the preacher.

The real question was Why now? Why had God waited until the last day to help Nickolai? Of course, Nickolai knew the answer to that question. God wanted to remove all doubt from Nickolai's mind that there was anything he could do himself to work out his own miracle story.

Chapter 28

A nd so the morning flew by. By noon they had already made five trips. Nickolai was speechless. What could he say? God was performing an astonishing miracle and doing it in a way that Nickolai could never have predicted.

All afternoon the two of them hustled. Nickolai grew weary from his continual running after the ox and cart. It was almost ridiculous. All week he had been trying to get the ox to run, but he had failed miserably.

Now he was the one running just to keep up with the ox, and it was wearing him out. After his regular trips to the box, his muscles had truly atrophied, but that was another incredible part about this whole amazing miracle. Nickolai had energy and full use of his legs. True, his leg muscles were no longer tough and sinewy as they had once been, but he was keeping up, and his legs weren't failing him. There was something to be said for that!

Although he was growing bone-weary and short of breath, he would not allow himself to ride in the cart, even if just out to the spring with empty barrels. He knew he just couldn't take the chance of wearing the ox out. Old Maksim had to be nearing the breaking point! How could he sustain that speed and intensity for all these hours?

Nickolai kept thinking that the ox would drop any minute, but he didn't—he just kept going and going and going. It was nothing short of a miracle indeed! Without a shadow of a doubt, nothing short of God's Spirit was keeping the ox on his feet.

It was all so exciting how things had transpired. Nickolai

dared not stop for fear they would somehow lose the momentum Maksim had gained. By the time the shadows of late afternoon had turned to evening, they had completed seven trips to the spring. They needed to make only one last trip.

Would they make it by sunset? Was Nickolai pressing his luck at taking Maksim out one more time?

Fortunately, Maksim had his own ideas. When Nickolai turned the cart around and paused to check the angle of the sun in the sky, the ox headed out of camp without hesitation.

Nickolai was famished, but he had no choice. He had to follow. He had managed to grab a loaf of bread when he drove by the kitchen about noon, but that was all he had gotten to eat.

That last trip to the spring was the hardest of all. It seemed to Nickolai that it would never end. By now Maksim had slowed a bit, but the stop at the spring gave him a much-needed rest. He drank long and deep at the spring as he had so many times already that day.

But when Nickolai put the lids on the barrels and turned the cart around, Maksim took off just like every other trip. Again Nickolai had to run to keep up, but they both had their second wind now, and it was as if nothing could deter them. God had truly blessed them with a will and the energy to succeed. The Sabbath rest was looking really good by now.

Never in his life had he looked forward so much to resting on the Lord's holy day! Never had he been so sure that God was working behind the scenes to perform a miracle to end all miracles! And all for the sake of a Russian pastor who had dedicated himself to honor God and His memorial of Creation.

As they raced across the steppes of the Siberian plain, the shadows lengthened even farther. Many creatures were stirring for the evening now. The lemmings were gathering by the score on the hummocks of sedge grass, squeaking and chattering their rodent talk. A lone snowy owl again eyed them from his perch of tundra sod. And on the rise to the north, a half dozen Russian prairie wolves were sitting, waiting for the moon to come up. They watched with interest as the man and ox raced by, the cart bumping and jostling along.

Amazingly enough, Nickolai never even gave the wolves a thought. Ordinarily he might have been afraid of their numbers, and maybe he should have been, but honestly, he really didn't have the time to dilly-dally. He had a Sabbath to prepare for, and the camp was just in sight around the bend. This was not a time to be afraid of a wolf attack. God had performed a miracle for the preacher and the ox, and right now Nickolai was sure 100 wolves would not have been able to detain them.

Maksim pulled in to camp, his legs still trotting. Only when the cart pulled up to the kitchen did his legs stop churning. Only then did the man allow himself to stop and catch his breath.

There sat the other eight full barrels of water, waiting to be used the next day. The sun hadn't quite yet set, but it was very near to doing so. With God's help Nickolai had completed the impossible task that he had set out to do.

As he slid the barrels down the skid ramps set against the cart, Nickolai bowed his head and breathed a sigh of relief. The miracle was complete! There was no other explanation for the job they had been able to accomplish! God had truly done His part.

In the far-reaching shadows of the waning day, a well-known verse came to Nickolai's mind. "Not by might nor by power, but by My Spirit, says the Lord of hosts" (Zechariah 4:6, NKJV).

Never in Nickolai's life had a verse of Scripture held such meaning. Never had a text been so rich with significance. Truly Nickolai had triumphed over the test that had threatened to undo his faith, and the victory was sweeter than anything he had experienced or ever imagined.

Chapter 29

The last rays of the late-setting summer sun were cutting across the landscape as Nickolai took Maksim to the stable. He hurriedly unhooked Maksim from the cart and pulled the harness from his neck and shoulders. Then he gave the tired ox some sedge grass and slapped him on the rump.

"I want you to enjoy this rest, Maksim. You deserve it!" He stepped to the stable doorway, and then turned to the old ox one last time. "I hope you know I won't be coming for you tomorrow morning. We don't have to work at all tomorrow. We've earned a rest—both of us—and we're going to get it."

Nickolai went to one of the water barrels, scooped some water out with a wooden bucket, and headed back to the barracks. It was time for a good bath.

When he was dressed in the only other shirt and pair of clothes he owned, he went to the kitchen for something to eat before Petya closed the kitchen for the night. As usual, he was late for supper, but as usual, Petya had a bowl of borsch waiting for him. He also had a side order of Russian black bread and a rare slab of cheese.

"Well, this is a delicacy!" Nickolai smiled as he savored a bite of the yellow cheese. "Where'd you get it? It's got to be the best treat I've seen in camp yet."

"An old man who lives not far from here has a few reindeer he's tamed. He milks some of the does, and then makes cheese. I was surprised," the cook added, cutting off a thin slice of the cheese for himself. "It does taste pretty good for reindeer cheese, but then again I've never eaten reindeer cheese before, so I guess I don't know what it's supposed to taste like."

After supper Nickolai ambled over to the warden's office to give him the news. He had managed to haul the needed water barrels for the Sabbath hours.

The warden looked up from his desk in surprise. "You've got 10 barrels in camp right now full of water?"

"Yes, sir." Nickolai tried not to sound too happy. He didn't want the warden to think of some extra task he might need done. *That would be a dirty trick, even for the warden,* Nickolai thought.

"Very well, then, Panchuk. Go on and rest. You deserve it. I understand you've been putting in some pretty late nights." The warden turned back to what he had been doing.

"Oh, and Panchuk," he added as he stared at Nickolai over the top of his horn-rimmed glasses, "what was with the ox today? They told me the animal was going wild on you. Wouldn't stop running."

Nickolai smiled sheepishly. "Yes, sir, he was a bit overwrought."

"Overwrought!" the warden nearly burst out laughing. "According to everyone who saw him, he was more like— crazy!"

"Yes, sir, I'd have to agree with you there. A bit crazy. I can't account for it, but he was—well, we'll just say God helped us get the water in."

How could Nickolai explain what he really thought? That God had spooked the old ox? Or put a bug in his ear? Or given him a shot of adrenaline that had lasted all day?

Perhaps he should have told the warden more about the power of his God. Perhaps, but then it didn't matter, because the warden didn't really want to know and was waving him off.

And so the Sabbath began for Nickolai. He didn't flaunt his time off. Instead he stayed inside the barracks and prayed most of the day. The other prisoners all went to their work assignments, so he had the time to himself. Even the guards left him alone.

Over and over he thanked God for the miracle performed on his behalf. God had indeed done a marvelous thing, and He had done it with a dumb ox. The whole thing reminded Nickolai of the story in the Bible in which God had used a donkey to be His mouthpiece.

The donkey hadn't really wanted to be part of the whole adventure. But like Maksim, he had been drawn unwittingly into the grand plot of the story when Balaam decided to disobey God. On the road to Moab an angel of God tried to prevent Balaam and his donkey from going on a mission to curse Israel. Balaam didn't know that, of course, and he gave the donkey the beating of its life. The poor old donkey put up quite a fuss and then started talking.

Nickolai thought about the similarities between Maksim and Balaam's donkey. Like Balaam's donkey, Maksim had been used by God to be His witness. Like the donkey, Maksim was part of a wonderful miracle that might very well be told down through the years of time.

The day turned out to be a grand day for rest and relaxation for Nickolai, and he enjoyed the fruit of his labors with relish. He couldn't remember when he had felt a more complete peace. And he slept some. He deserved it, he felt, for all the nights of short sleep, and for having to run behind the oxcart all day on Friday. He figured that he had run some 15 or 16 miles (24 or 25 kilometers).

Nickolai went to the mess hall somewhere near sunset. All of the men had already eaten when he arrived, so Petya let him come back into the kitchen and eat there so they could talk.

Chapter 30

Is it true?" the cook asked, a gleam of admiration in his eye.

Nickolai smiled humbly. "You mean about old Maksim?"

"Exactly. I know you got your quota of barrels, but I also heard that you brought in eight cartloads of water in one day."

Nickolai shrugged his shoulders and kept on smiling.

"That's 16 barrels of water, preacher man!" Nickolai knew Petya wasn't making fun. The name sounded more like a term of endearment coming from Petya.

"That's right. It's more than I ever managed before."

"Ha!" Petya grunted. "I hear it's a record! More than anyone ever hauled in one day!"

"That so?" Nickolai knew he had to share the whole story with Petya. He couldn't let Petya think that it had been his doing—or even old Maksim's, for that matter. If anyone would understand, Petya would.

"I can't take credit for all that water I hauled yesterday."

Petya stared at him with raised eyebrows.

"That's right. You see, I'm a man of prayer, Petya. After those two years in the box, I learned to depend on God for everything. He helped me deal with the pain and hunger. He gave me peace of mind when I needed it most. And I thank Him especially for life. I owe Him my life, many times over."

"So your God helped you haul all that water? How did He do that?"

"By giving old Maksim super amounts of stamina and energy and inspiration. Strength enough to go all day, running constantly without even stopping to eat. And inspiration to do it in the first place. A little water and a few carrots I brought along for him was all he had."

Petya shook his head. "Well, I did find the part about the ox almost unbelievable. Does the warden know all this?"

"I don't think so. I didn't tell him. He didn't ask."

Petya sat on a stool staring at Nickolai. "Did you ask God to do that for you?"

"I didn't ask Him to do that specifically for me, because I didn't know it was possible." Nickolai shook his head. "But I did ask my God to please help me find some way to haul enough water so that I wouldn't have to work on the Sabbath."

"So your God came up with this, huh? Pretty neat!" Petya looked pensive. "Does your God help everyone who asks?"

"Everyone who comes to Him in faith. Everyone who seeks Him with all their heart, and soul, and mind."

"And that's what you do?"

"As a Christian pastor, I must say I have always done that. By His grace."

There was silence in the kitchen for quite some time. The only sound that could be heard was the sound of the hot kitchen stove popping and snapping as it slowly cooled for the night.

"Would He do such a thing for me?" Petya asked earnestly, and Nickolai could hardly believe his ears. Here was a man wanting God to come into his life and touch him. This man was asking the essential question of every seeker who had ever come to Jesus—"What must I do to be saved?"

Nickolai went to bed that night, inspired and energized for another week. What the week would bring was anybody's guess, but one thing was for sure: he would have more time this week so he wouldn't have to kill himself or Maksim. He wouldn't have to run the ox into the ground every day to get the water he would need. This week he would need to bring in 70 barrels of water in six days.

Earlier than usual the next morning, Nickolai was in the barn hitching Maksim up to the cart. But strangely enough Maksim was in no hurry to get going. It was as if all the energy had gone out of his bones, as if he had used up Sunday's energy supply on Friday. Try as he might, Nickolai was powerless to get old Maksim going.

By the end of the day they had managed to bring in only 10 barrels of water, and they had to work after dark to do it.

Monday was no better. It seemed that the harder Nickolai pushed Maksim, the slower he moved. Did the old ox know something Nickolai didn't? Was he playing some kind of silly game just to pit his wits against the man? Was it some kind of a standoff again, where Maksim did what he wanted, when he wanted?

Or was it nothing of the sort? Had the previous Friday just been a freak accident of nature? Had it been an incredible, unexplainable phenomenon of animal behavior that no one had ever seen and would never see again?

Nickolai had hoped that on Tuesday he might make up for the loads he had failed to haul on the first two days of the week. But Tuesday was a bust too, and the outcome worried Nickolai, leaving him feeling frustrated and confused.

He was now getting up so early every morning that he had to wonder if he was losing all touch with reality. What kind of life was this? He was going to bed at night after everyone else, and then getting up before anyone in camp had even stirred. By dawn he and Maksim were usually already on their way to the spring.

On Wednesday they made some progress. Old Maksim seemed to have new life in his step once again, and he moved with purpose all that morning.

By midafternoon it was clear to Nickolai that they would be able to bring in at least seven loads. That was an extra four barrels toward his goal of 10. Nickolai was still holding out hope that there might be a chance of filling his quota by Friday night.

Maksim was moving with a purpose now, and he didn't let up all day. Nickolai felt so good about the rate at which they were working now that he found himself singing an old hymn. "'O God, our help in ages past, our hope for years to come, our shelter from the stormy blast, and our eternal home. Under the shadow of Thy throne still may we dwell secure; sufficient is Thine arm alone, and our defense is sure.'"

Nickolai could feel the power of the Holy Spirit beside him out there on the lonely road to the spring. He raised his hands to the sky as he sang the final verse of the old hymn in a throaty baritone voice.

"'O God, our help in ages past, our hope for years to come; be Thou our guide while life shall last, and our eternal home.'"

Nickolai went to bed that night feeling that the day had been a success, but he secretly dreaded the coming of another day. What chance did he have of making the quota? If he could somehow haul seven loads the next day, it would be their only hope. Seven loads on Thursday would give them a total of eight barrels toward the extra 10 they needed, but he knew they could haul no less. Even so, that would still leave them with another six trips needed on Friday.

Unfortunately, Thursday was a bomb again. Maksim was back to his old tricks of poking along the windswept road to the spring. If the situation hadn't seemed so serious to Nickolai, he might have taken the time to feel sorry for the old ox. Now all he had time for was exasperation.

At the end of the long day they had managed to bring in a measly 10 barrels. They had made only five trips, two trips short of his goal. They were now six extra barrels short of the tally they would need to bring in by Friday sunset.

And with that realization, still far short of their goal, all of Nickolai's hopes died.

Chapter 31

On Friday morning Nickolai didn't even bother to get out of bed early. What was the point? It wouldn't be possible for them to finish the job by sunset anyway. There were just too many barrels of water to bring into camp by the time the Sabbath would begin.

It didn't seem to matter that Nickolai had prayed and worked hard all week again, stretching every fiber of his being to add to the number of barrels needed. It had all been for nothing.

Finally, just after dawn, Nickolai got up and headed for the kitchen. There was no sense of urgency now. He could afford to get some breakfast this morning.

On his way to the kitchen, another prisoner called out to him. "You'd better go to the stables and check on that old ox. I think he's gone crazy! He's making a lot of racket in there!"

Nickolai stopped in his tracks. He wanted to ignore the man's announcement, but a faint hope of something a week old flickered in his heart. It wasn't possible was it? Could Maksim be thinking of trying to run a repeat performance?

Nickolai turned and headed for the stables, and the closer he got, the more optimistic he became. Old Maksim was indeed going berserk, if that was really him making all the noise! It sounded as if he was trying to pull the stable down, posts and all!

"I don't believe it!" Nickolai yelled, rushing through the open stable door. There stood Maksim, yanking on his chain and pawing at the ground impatiently.

Nickolai surveyed the scene for only a moment, and

then he flew into action. If old Maksim wanted to haul water barrels, then that is what they would do. It was later than Nickolai would have liked it to be, and he wished with all his heart now that he had gotten up by faith and done his part. But he had not, and so he had to make up for the hour or so he had wasted in bed—if God would be so merciful.

It was a strange and almost comical feeling Nickolai had as he hurriedly unhooked Maksim from his chain, threw the harness over his neck and shoulders, and hitched him to the oxcart. All week he had worked early and late to accomplish his purpose. It had been all he could think of day and night.

But then when things didn't turn out as he had planned, his faith had floundered, and he had lost sight of the goal. What a shame—Nickolai scolded himself over and over! Now, when he desperately needed to be up and on his way, he had been sleeping on the job.

"Forgive me, Lord," he fervently prayed. "I'm not worthy of Your goodness. Help me to make up for the lost time. Help Maksim to do his part—he's more worthy of Your grace than I am."

Nickolai heaved a sigh as he checked the rope that held the barrels securely in place. Sometimes dumb animals weren't so dumb. At least they knew how to listen to God's voice. He thought about the story of Balaam and his donkey again and how God had worked though the actions of an animal. When Balaam couldn't see God's will, a willing donkey had.

And now it appeared God was ready to use Maksim again. The ox was willing—it was the man who lacked the faith.

In short order they were off to the spring. If anyone had been watching, they would have seen the ox running full tilt out of camp, his tail flying and the cart bouncing along behind him, and the man running for all he was worth to keep up. It was as if the ox were on a mission, and indeed he was. No longer did it appear as if the man were in charge.

Clearly the ox was in control and determining the pace at which they would work.

On and on he ran as if in a frenzy, as if he had somehow lost his mind. Again Nickolai felt it was the strangest thing he had ever seen. It was as if the angels had built a fire under old Maksim and ignited his spirit to fulfill God's will and greatest wish—that Nickolai be rewarded for his desire to honor God's holy Sabbath. All week it had been Nickolai who had been pushing them hard to bring extra barrels of water to the kitchen, always mindful that they needed a tally of 70 in order to make the mark. And all week Maksim had done his part, but more often than not he had worked with less energy than Nickolai wished he would.

Now it was Friday again, the preparation day, and Maksim was on a mission. The trip to the spring for that first load of water was run in record time. It was not a complete surprise that Maksim was running helter-skelter to and from the spring. Nickolai had witnessed him acting this way the previous Friday, but it was a shock that he was doing it for the second week in a row. It helped to remove any doubt in Nickolai's mind that such a thing might have been a freak accident the week before. As Nickolai ran panting behind the cart all the way back to camp, he had to admit that God works in mysterious ways.

As everyone in camp watched Nickolai and Maksim, it confirmed in their minds, even more than the week before, that the God of heaven was again working on Nickolai's behalf. How else could it be interpreted?

Since entering the camp, Nickolai had been a living testimony of determination and loyalty. The colors of his character were beginning to become obvious to everyone, prisoners and guards alike. Even the warden had been forced to admit that here was a man of the highest caliber, one who would rather suffer persecution and pain than dishonor the God he served.

And now again, they were witnessing a miracle in action,

evidence of the power that God was willing to demonstrate on Nickolai's behalf. It was a strange and unusual sight, man and ox running full speed into camp, the oxcart rolling along with two full barrels of water on board. And it was equally bizarre to see Maksim turn the oxcart around and head back to the spring as soon as the full water barrels were taken off and the empty ones dropped into place.

And then the whole performance would repeat itself again as man and beast were seen speeding out of camp and across the wide-open spaces of the Siberian steppes.

Chapter 32

All that morning Nickolai and Maksim worked, sweat pouring from their bodies. It was an amazing and almost comical sight! As the two could be seen approaching the camp, someone would always signal their arrival with a shout, "Here they come again!"

And then everyone within range would stop whatever it was they were doing—prisoners and guards alike. Petya would always come out of the kitchen for a look. It was a great way to take a break. By the time Nickolai and Maksim returned to the camp the third time, everyone was cheering and throwing their caps into the air.

Nickolai hardly had time to notice their shouts of encouragement. He did give a tired salute on his entry into camp, and then another wave of his arm again as the cart spun around to make its next trip to the spring.

If Nickolai had been watching on the fourth trip back to camp, he would have noticed that even the warden had stopped what he was doing to come out and see the amazing spectacle.

By noon they were already heading out for their fifth trip to the spring. As Nickolai hurried to catch up with the ox, Petya ran alongside him and handed him a small bag with cold turnips and Russian black bread in it. Nickolai had managed to drink a little water each time they stopped at the spring and the camp, but he had not thought of eating. Now he realized that he was famished, and he was so grateful for the friendship of this man who was watching out for him.

He ate the turnips as he ran, praying that God would

help the food to digest in spite of the conditions in which he was eating the meal.

On the return trip Nickolai saw four or five of the prairie wolves come out and sit in a row to watch the man and ox race by. He tossed a chunk of the black bread to the wolves and watched them fight over it as the cart raced away to the east.

The miles became easier to run, and his breathing less strenuous. It was as though God was giving Nickolai a second and third wind, so he could become part of the miracle in action.

The day melted away as trip after trip was made, until there was only one last run. By now the man and beast were running in tandem, as though this adventure had turned them into a well-oiled machine.

And they finished the task with time to spare. By the time the sun dipped below the western horizon, Nickolai had unloaded the last barrel of water, gone to the barracks to clean up, and was on his way to the kitchen to eat the evening meal he knew Petya would have waiting for him there.

What a day it had been, and what a lesson in faith for Nickolai. In his heart he knew that he would never again doubt God's amazing watchcare and His ability to come to the aid of a soul in need. Of course Nickolai believed in the power of God to protect and preserve, and he knew of God's willingness to act on behalf of His children in time of need. But he had never experienced such a dramatic display of God's power to vindicate one of His children. And to everyone in camp this had been a clear demonstration of the lengths to which Nickolai's God would go to honor the pastor for his faithfulness.

As Nickolai sat in the kitchen eating a hot bowl of borsch and sipping a cup of tea, the cook spoke of the electricity that had ignited the camp.

"You did it again!" Petya exclaimed. "It was amazing!"

"We did it!" Nickolai countered. "Maksim and I did it,

and we owe it to God, from whom all blessings flow."

Petya shook his head in disbelief. "I wish you could have seen the two of you!" he crowed. "What a sight!" He handed Nickolai another slice of black bread. "You two are like celebrities here in camp now. I don't suppose the warden will ever give you trouble again. He can't. The guards won't let him!"

On his way back to the barracks Nickolai stopped to watch the moon rising in the east. The orange oval of light looked warm and inviting, like the feeling he had in his chest. For the first time since arriving in camp more than two years ago, he felt exhilaratingly free.

And God was responsible for it. It had taken awhile for Nickolai to see his prayers fully realized, but in the end things had worked out for the best, with God being justified and Nickolai feeling vindicated. Nickolai decided that it was always best to trust fully in God's timing, because only God could see the end from the beginning.

As Nickolai turned to enter the barracks, he could hear the prairie wolves howling somewhere in the distant darkness, but the sound no longer made him feel lonely. He remembered feeling lost and forlorn when he had first arrived in camp. The sound of the prairie wolves had left him feeling empty, and he had even been tempted to feel abandoned by God. But not any longer.

Clearer than ever before was his faith in Jesus. It was a moment of truth for him, and it thrilled him through and through to know that God was with him even on the wastelands of the Siberian tundra. To have a peace like that was truly worth dying for, but of course it didn't look as if that was what God required now. He had stood the test, and he had come through shining.

Chapter 33

Nickolai reaped the benefits of the second Friday miracle even more than he had the first. Again he spent time in prayer, thanking God for His wonderful gift of rest on the holy Sabbath day. Again he had a chance to escape his labors of the week.

All that following week Nickolai and Maksim worked together to bring the needed water to the camp. And all that week, strangely enough, Maksim worked at a normal pace.

It was amazing! The slow pace at which Maksim persisted in working Sundays through Thursdays was almost as phenomenal as his working to beat the band on Friday. But by Friday sunset, the extra 10 barrels of water for the Sabbath were again ready and waiting at the kitchen. The whole thing was a spectacular miracle to Nickolai.

As the weeks passed, Nickolai and Maksim settled into their routine. Sundays through Thursdays always brought just a little bit of consternation to Nickolai. Why did Maksim have to poke along all week, and then run lickety-split on Fridays? What was he trying to prove? Didn't the ox ever learn? Or was that it at all? Was Maksim just operating, in fact, on the instinctive impressions the Holy Spirit was giving him?

But there was another thing. Nickolai always felt funny knowing that on Friday the ox would be performing his marathon run. It made him feel presumptuous and just a little bit guilty knowing that he could relax and just let God make the Friday miracle happen.

But it was out of Nickolai's hands, and apparently that's

the way God wanted it. In the final scope of things, Nickolai's worries had ended up being fairly redundant anyway. What was most important now was the fact that the man and ox were proving to be a real witness at the prison camp.

The weather turned cooler in August, with more rain falling than Nickolai remembered from previous years. Many days he had to work in the rain, and he suffered from the dampness of it all. Some days the rain turned to sleet and ice, and on the days it didn't rain, frost fell thick and hard. Petya lent him a raincoat, for which Nickolai was grateful. What would he have done without such a friend?

After work many evenings, Nickolai spent time talking to Petya. Sometimes they talked in the kitchen, sometimes in the barracks. Sometimes they talked late into the night. But they talked less and less of prison life, and more and more about eternal things.

One evening in the kitchen Petya came right to the point. "You've been such an inspiration to me since you came to this camp. You've suffered so much for God, and yet you are still faithful to Him. I'm so inspired by the hope you've brought us all." Petya stared at the floor solemnly. "Can you help me find this peace you carry with you everywhere you go? I want the power of this peace in my life too."

Nickolai laid his hand on Petya's shoulder. "Believe in the Lord Jesus Christ," he said. "If you do this, you'll have God's peace when you need it most."

"You've said that before," Petya raised his eyes to stare at Nickolai unbelievingly. "Can it be true that it's really that simple?"

"God has made it simple, Petya. He's not willing that anyone should perish. Trust me on this one. It's the one thing that has always given me courage to live for Him every day." Nickolai rubbed his tired eyes.

Petya blew out the kerosene lamp, and then closed the door to the kitchen. As the two men stepped out into the night, the moon was full, rising quickly from the horizon.

the dark several hours before dawn each morning, and then three or four hours again after sunset.

The ice was forming thick at the spring now, and Nickolai had to use an ax to cut through it. Of course, this took time and made the trips longer, but Nickolai had other things to worry about.

In the cold, dark hours of the winter, Nickolai knew he needed to be watchful of the wolves. Food was scarce now on the tundra, so a man and an ox might prove tempting to their hungry stomachs.

But God was merciful, and although Nickolai and Maksim had a few scares, they managed to stay alive and well.

The cold, hard winter passed somehow, and then spring gave way to summer. By now Nickolai had accepted the fact that he might be in this prison camp for a very long time. When he was tempted to wonder why God needed him in this remote tundra outpost, he remembered Petya's decision for Jesus.

And he contemplated the salvation of the other 300 men who were imprisoned at the camp. More than anything he wanted them to know God as he did. Eventually he started Bible studies with those who were interested, and before long there was a small band that met regularly.

For seven more years Nickolai spent his days at the remote prison camp on the steppes of Siberia. For seven years he worked with Maksim to haul water from the spring. For all those years he remained a constant witness to the power of God in the life of a dedicated Christian.

To the men in camp, the life and work of Nickolai and Maksim became a living testimony. Visitors who came to camp witnessed the phenomenon themselves. Those who left the prison told of a man and ox that ran all day every Friday so that they could rest all day Saturday.

And then one day the army officer who had freed Nickolai from the crate came back to the prison camp. When he saw Nickolai and Maksim hauling water, he remembered the incident from eight years before.

But now the colonel was told quite a different story. When he heard about Maksim's strange habit of running all day Friday to bring in a two-day supply of water in one, he was amazed.

With great interest he asked Nickolai about the operation, and Nickolai shared the whole incredible tale. He told how desperate he had been those first few weeks trying to get Maksim to haul enough water fast enough to earn a Sabbath day's rest. And of course he told how good God had been to him. He explained how the ordeal had tested his faith in God, and how he had almost given up.

The miracle of Maksim's marathon run that first Friday stirred the colonel's heart, and the repeat performance the following Friday was even more surprising to him. The colonel could see that Nickolai was a good man. He could see clearly now that the preacher had not been guilty of insubordination. In fact, the testimony of his daily life was proof that he had been willing all along to do whatever was asked of him. Most important, the colonel saw that Nickolai had been faithful to his God. Without a doubt he had been willing to do whatever his God had asked of him.

The colonel then shocked Nickolai by taking him to the warden's office to announce that he was going to sign his release forms. He was free to go home on the train to be with his family once again.

"You have shown us all what a man of character can do if he is motivated," the colonel said proudly. "And you have shown what devotion can do for a man who loves his God."

The colonel chuckled, and then added, "I guess none of us have ever seen an animal as crazy as your ox. If you and your God can get a stubborn ox to run like that, you could probably do just about anything!"

With tears in his eyes Nickolai thanked the colonel for his kindness. And then he took his few personal belongings, followed the colonel and his horse back to the train, and began the long journey back to Kiev.

Nickolai returned to the life of a pastor and continued to witness for God during the good times as he had during the bad. His church members rejoiced with him that God had brought him home from his long ordeal, and they thanked Jesus for his faithfulness under fire.

Today, like every other Seventh-day Adventist Christian in the former Soviet Union, Nickolai Panchuk waits for Jesus to come again. One day soon he will see Jesus coming in the clouds of heaven and hear the words "Well done, My good and faithful servant. You have been faithful to Me in small things and in big. You have suffered for My sake. Come and enter into the joy of your Lord" (see Matthew 25:21).

Chapter 35

But that's not the end of the story. After Nickolai left for home, a new prisoner came to camp who knew nothing of the man and ox who ran all day on Fridays so that they could rest on Saturdays.

The new man, Gennadi, was also given the job of hauling water from the spring every day, and he quickly learned to plod along behind the oxcart. Like Nickolai, he knew that the job was the one most hated by all the men in camp. No one else wanted to do all that walking.

However, he also discovered that Maksim was stubborn and would refuse to do anything that was not part of his regular regiment. The old ox refused to be hurried. He refused to be intimidated. He refused to continue working after dark.

Not surprisingly, Gennadi soon came to admit that he wasn't the one in charge while on their trips to the spring. Maksim obviously was. They were up at the crack of dawn every day, plodding laboriously back and forth to the spring, but always on Maksim's own terms.

But on that first Friday morning, Gennadi was in for the surprise of his life. The old ox fairly ran his legs off all day, and Gennadi was so shocked he didn't know what to think.

No one had bothered beforehand to tell him about Maksim's strange habits, or his famous track record. Maybe it was because they wanted to see the look on Gennadi's face when he finally witnessed it for himself. Maybe they were looking forward to hearing the new driver rant on and on about how crazy the old ox was. Maybe it was just that the whole thing had been going on for so long now that they never thought about it as a strange and unusual event anymore.

But on that first Friday morning as Maksim came running back into camp, Gennadi came huffing and puffing along behind him. The poor prisoner looked as though he had been running a race. When he finally came to a stop, he bent over with his hands on his knees, wheezing and desperately trying to catch his breath. Perspiration dripped from his face, and his clothes were completely soaked with sweat.

But if he thought he was going to get a rest, he was in for a second surprise. Maksim never really gave Gennadi time to get his breathing back to normal. No sooner were the water barrels unloaded from the cart than the old ox took off again in a cloud of dust.

And that was the last anyone saw of them until more than an hour later, when they came racing back down the road into camp again. This time Gennadi was even farther behind.

Who would have thought that an ox pulling a cart full of water barrels would outdo a man running on foot? Of course, Maksim was used to this—he had been doing it for more than eight years now.

The two of them went at it all morning. On the ride out to the spring Gennadi jumped on the cart for a rest. However, when the cart had two full barrels on it, he had to run on foot all the way back. Each time they came racing back into camp, Gennadi would take a few moments to rest, but he knew he dared not wait too long for fear the ox would take off for the spring again with the full water barrels still on the cart.

By late afternoon Gennadi looked as though he had been running a marathon, and it appeared he would drop from exhaustion any moment. He might never have made it through the afternoon had Petya not come to his aid the last few trips to help him unload the full water barrels from the cart.

"What's wrong with that animal?" Gennadi would shout every time he came stumbling into camp. "He's going to kill me!"

Of course, everyone just laughed, because they knew the rest of the story and were having their fun at Gennadi's expense.

But by the end of the day Gennadi could take it no longer. As the sun neared its resting place below the horizon and old Maksim had pulled the bumping cart into camp for the last time, Gennadi slumped to the ground, his back against the wheel of the oxcart.

"I give up!" he panted and closed his eyes as Petya and several other men gathered around. "The ox is possessed!" he rasped, putting his hands to his head. "There's no other explanation!"

"Yes, there is," a voice sounded nearby, and Gennadi turned to see the warden standing behind them.

The warden paused for effect. "You see, that preacher from Kiev has been training old Maksim for years. Nickolai Panchuk refused to work on the seventh day of every week, and he's spoiled the ox with that business of his. Ruined him, and he'll never be the same!"

The warden looked around the circle of men and then directly at Gennadi. "There's no doubt about it in my mind. That preacher made a Sabbathkeeper of the ox."

And truly he had. Old Maksim had turned into a seventh-day ox. But it hadn't really been any of Nickolai's doing. The preacher had run side by side with Maksim all those years to bring enough water to last through the Sabbath. And it had always taken a marathon Friday to finish the job each week.

The credit for such a phenomenon was all God's, of course, and everyone who wanted to know the truth had been told so by Nickolai.

Even after Nickolai had left the prison camp and returned home to his family, the influence of his holy life lived on through the testimony of an ox. Old Maksim continued to be true to his duties, ready to be used by his Creator as a witness for the Sabbath.

Nickolai Panchuk was gone, but when there was no one left to share the gospel story, there was still Maksim, the seventh-day ox.

FREE Lessons at www.BibleStudies.com

Call:
1-888-456-7933

Write:
Discover
P.O. Box 999
Loveland, CO 80539-0999

It's easy to learn more about the Bible!